Defending Hope

Defending Hope

Semiotics and Intertextuality in 1 Peter

Justin Langford

WIPF & STOCK · Eugene, Oregon

DEFENDING HOPE
Semiotics and Intertextuality in 1 Peter

Copyright © 2013 Justin Langford. All rights reserved. Except for brief quotations in critical publications or reviews, no part of this book may be reproduced in any manner without prior written permission from the publisher. Write: Permissions, Wipf and Stock Publishers, 199 W. 8th Ave., Suite 3, Eugene, OR 97401.

Wipf & Stock
An Imprint of Wipf and Stock Publishers
199 W. 8th Ave., Suite 3
Eugene, OR 97401

www.wipfandstock.com

ISBN 13: 978-1-62032-547-6

Manufactured in the U.S.A.

To Melinda
for all your love, encouragement, support, and sacrifice
and to Noah, London, and Reilly
for the constant joy you bring into my life

Contents

List of Illustrations | viii
Preface | ix
Abbreviations | xi
Introduction | xiii

1 Semiotics and Biblical Interpretation | 1
2 A New Approach to Intertextuality | 26
3 The Textual Universe of 1 Peter | 53
4 Opening the Encyclopedia of 1 Peter | 86
5 "Signs" of Hope in 1 Peter | 97
  Conclusion | 127

Bibliography | 131

Illustrations

Figures

1. Eco's Representation of the Sign Triad | 37
2. Story and Hope in 1 Peter | 82

Tables

1. Peirce's Sign Trichotomies | 38
2. A Comparison of Epistolary Outlines of 1 Peter | 59
3. A Comparison of Rhetorical Outlines of 1 Peter | 64
4. Isaiah 40:6–8 in 1 Peter 1:24–25 | 100
5. Isaiah 28:16 in 1 Peter 2:6 | 103
6. Isaiah 8:14 in 1 Peter 2:8 | 105
7. Isaiah 43:20–21 in 1 Peter 2:9 | 106
8. Isaiah 53:9 in 1 Peter 2:22 | 108
9. Isaiah 8:12–13 in 1 Peter 3:14–15 | 110
10. Isaiah 11:2 in 1 Peter 4:14 | 112
11. Isaiah 48:10 in 1 Peter 1:7 | 114
12. Isaiah 52:3 in 1 Peter 1:18 | 116
13. Isaiah 28:16 in 1 Peter 2:4 | 117
14. Isaiah 10:3 in 1 Peter 2:12 | 118
15. Isaiah 53 in 1 Peter 2:23–25 | 121
16. Isaianic Signs in 1 Peter | 125

Preface

FIVE YEARS AGO, ALMOST to the day, I embarked on a formal academic study of biblical intertexuality. My interest was primarily in the New Testament use of the Old Testament, specifically in relation to how meaning was defined. Gradually, this interest morphed into a passion for intertextual studies as a whole. Throughout my research I was introduced to various seminal figures in critical literary theory who approached intertextuality much differently than the biblical scholars I was reading. This piqued my interest, and before I knew it I was immersed in the writings of individuals such as Julia Kristeva, Roland Barthes, and Mikhail Bakhtin. I quickly discovered that among those literary theorists practicing intertextuality, there were variations on how this task was to be accomplished. In the process of researching this methodological dilemma, I encountered a German New Testament scholar, Stefan Alkier, who proposed that semiotics was a valid solution to this methodological problem. He based his work squarely on the writings of the American philosopher Charles Sanders Peirce. Alkier's work launched me into the dense, yet insightful, practical, and philosophical writings of Peirce. After reading Peirce, I found myself reflecting on the initial question of meaning and communication. As a result of all this study, you are now reading the Preface of a revised version of my doctoral dissertation.

Although my interest in intertextuality has been the focus of my doctoral research over the past five years, this interest was birthed out of a long-time fascination with how the biblical authors were utilizing other texts of the biblical canon. Therefore, I decided to publish this book for two primary reasons. First, the topic of "intertextuality" or "the New Testament use of the Old Testament" is one that laypeople are interested in today. They are asking the sort of questions that we in the academic guild are addressing. Since this book is not targeted to a lay audience, my hope is that

Defending Hope

academicians will see the value in a semiotic approach to intertextuality and seek to communicate this topic on a level where a lay audience can be engaged. I have confidence that this book provides a platform for broadening this conversation beyond academic circles. Second, biblical intertextuality is in need of a centralized approach that firmly organizes its efforts on a common theoretical basis. Semiotics has the potential of being such an approach. Of course, it is up to the academic guild as to whether this potentiality can become reality. Since my focus in this book is narrow—the use of Isaiah in 1 Peter—much more investigation and experimentation with the method is a necessity.

The completion of my doctoral dissertation was greatly aided by the encouragement and support of numerous individuals. First, I would like to express the deepest gratitude to all my major professors in New Testament studies at New Orleans Baptist Theological Seminary. Dr. Bill Warren, Dr. Gerald Stevens, Dr. Charlie Ray, and Dr. Craig Price have played vital roles in my academic development and in shaping my thinking about the New Testament. I thank Dr. Charlie Ray for his constructive guidance in my dissertation research and for being a dialogue partner with me on issues regarding intertextuality. Words cannot express my deep gratitude to Dr. Craig Price, my mentor and dear friend. He has pushed me toward excellence in all aspects of my academic work and my personal life, and he has instilled in me a love of 1 Peter and the apostle's message of hope. The encouragement, support, and sacrifice of my wife, Melinda, is too immeasurable to recount. I thank God for her daily and for our three precious children: Noah, London, and Reilly. They are a never-ending source of joy and pleasure, and they always challenge me to see things in new and fresh ways. I thank them for what they teach me and, more importantly, how they teach me.

I would like to express my appreciation to Indiana University Press for the kind courtesy they have extended to me to reproduce illustrations by Winfried Nöth and Umberto Eco (both illustrations are located in chapter 2). Finally, many thanks are due to the editorial staff at Wipf and Stock. It has been a joy to work alongside them to see this project through to its completion.

Abbreviations

Academic Sources

AB	Anchor Bible
ANTC	Abingdon New Testament Commentaries
BECNT	Baker Exegetical Commentary on the New Testament
BibInt	*Biblical Interpretation*
ConBOT	Coniectanea biblica: Old Testament Series
CritI	*Critical Inquiry*
EkklPh	*Ekklesiastikos Pharos*
FOTL	Forms of the Old Testament Literature
GBSNT	Guides to Biblical Scholarship: New Testament Series
HKAT	Handkommentar zum Alten Testament
HvTSt	*Hervormde teologiese studies*
IVPNTC	IVP New Testament Commentary Series
JBL	*Journal of Biblical Literature*
JP	*Journal of Philosophy*
JR	*Journal of Religion*
JSNTSup	Journal for the Study of the New Testament: Supplement Series
NCI	New Critical Idiom
NICNT	New International Commentary on the New Testament
NICOT	New International Commentary on the Old Testament

Defending Hope

NLH	*New Literary History*
NovTSup	Supplements to Novum Testamentum
NTL	New Testament Library
NTS	*New Testament Studies*
OTL	Old Testament Library
RTR	*Reformed Theological Review*
SBLDS	Society of Biblical Literature Dissertation Series
Scrip	*Scriptura*
Semeia	*Semeia*
SNTSMS	Society for New Testament Studies Monograph Series
WBC	Word Biblical Commentary
WUNT	Wissenschaftliche Untersuchungen zum Neuen Testament
ZNW	*Zeitschrift für die neutestamentliche Wissenschaft und die Kunde der älteren Kirche*

Academic Terms

LXX	Septuagint
MT	Masoretic Text
NT	New Testament
OG	Old Greek
OT	Old Testament

Introduction

IN THE REALM OF biblical studies, the term *intertextuality* is bandied about in scholarly literature and dialogue in a way that suggests a consensus exists on the definition of the term. On the contrary, scholars rarely agree on their definitions of intertextuality, although often a commonly held definition of the term is assumed. Even precise terms used within intertextual studies—such as *citation, quotation, allusion,* and *echo*—are defined variously. This terminological problem is only one half of the issue. The other, and that to which this book is devoted, is the methodological problem.

Current study of the New Testament (NT) is characterized by a frequently changing landscape of methodological approaches to the text. The presence of such numerous and diverse approaches points to a fundamental, and often assumed, belief that "no one interpretive method can claim to provide the one authentic meaning of a NT text."[1] Since intertextuality is a theory and not a method, often it is combined with other existing methodological approaches to the text. So what is true for the study of the NT generally is true for the study of intertextuality specifically: no agreed-upon method exists for approaching this realm of study. Furthermore, the variety of methods employed naturally yields a wide array of results when examining intertextual references in the NT. In this book, I offer a new approach to biblical intertextuality as a possible resolution to the methodological problem. This approach, based on semiotics, has the potential of resolving the methodological problem by providing a comprehensive framework for studying texts and their use of other texts.

Over the past thirty years, intertextual studies slowly have come to the fore as one of the major interpretive approaches to the biblical text. Such studies examine the relationship of one text to another. The approach itself can take place within the Old Testament (OT) and the NT and even

1. Green, *Hearing the New Testament*, 14.

across both testaments. For instance, intertextuality within the OT could investigate Isaiah's use of the Pentateuch. Intertextuality within the NT could examine the literary relationship between 2 Peter and Jude. Intertextuality across both testaments could investigate any use of the OT by the NT writers. The majority of intertextual research and scholarly debate has focused upon the latter of the three avenues. At this point, a description of the context out of which biblical intertextual studies has grown is necessary.

The term *intertextuality* did not have its genesis in biblical studies but in the realm of literary studies in the humanities.[2] *Intertextuality* was coined in the 1960s by the Bulgarian literary theorist and semiotician Julia Kristeva. She defined the term as the "transposition of one (or several) sign-system(s) into another."[3] Her definition demonstrates the integral role of semiotics (the study of signs and the sign process) for her view of intertextual analysis. Some of the key issues that accompanied Kristeva's description of her intertextual theory were the nature of texts, the production of meaning, and the role of the author and reader in the interpretive process. A fundamental assumption of this approach to intertextuality is that the meaning located within literary texts must be drawn out by the reader. Additionally, this assumption paved the way for modern literary theorists who view texts as lacking independent meaning and, thus, would argue for a form of reader-response approach to literary texts wherein meaning is derived solely from the interpreter.

One major contrast between secular intertextuality and biblical intertextuality is that Kristeva's conception of intertextuality specifically is a reaction to a conventional search for sources, whereas much of the early work done in biblical intertextuality was characterized by such source searching. Gradually, however, a shift has taken place in biblical intertextual studies from source-searching to an engagement with modern literary theory. While many other differences exist between secular intertextuality and biblical intertextuality, both disciplines do have one aspect in common: the term *intertextuality* is elusive in that usually it is defined inconsistently.

---

2. Strictly for the purpose of contrast, this form of intertextuality will be referred to hereafter as *secular* intertextuality.

3. Kristeva, *Revolution in Poetic Language*, 111. This article—which was first published as her thesis for the French *Doctorat d'Etat* in 1974—is Kristeva's systematic explanation of some of her earliest concepts that she developed in her linguistic studies in the 1960s. The term was introduced in her 1969 work *Séméiotikè: Recherches pour une sémanalyse*.

Introduction

For this study, intertextuality is defined as the dialogue between two or more independent texts, where a text is a verbal sign complex.

Biblical intertextuality falls within the purview of literary approaches to the biblical text. The fundamental assumption behind intertextual study is the belief that "no text exists in a vaccum."[4] Every text has some connection with other texts. Intertextuality specifically concerns itself with how texts relate to one another. The issues mentioned above regarding secular intertextual studies also are of great concern to scholars who engage in intertextual studies with regard to biblical literature. In particular, questions about the role of the author and the reader have spawned considerable debate among the scholarly community and have produced unique hermeneutical approaches to the text. The student of the NT cannot neglect these issues since an abundance of references to the OT are present in the NT. Indeed, all these issues comprise the fundamental objective of biblical studies in seeking the proper interpretation of the biblical text, including a determination as to which methods are valid for achieving this objective.

In relation to the methodological issue, two larger and all-encompassing questions must be addressed: What is the proper method for examining intertextual relationships between the NT and the OT? Does such a method account for issues of textuality and production of meaning (whether author-centered or reader-centered)? The answers to these two questions have been construed in various ways. Methodological applications of intertextuality range from a basic historical approach, which emphasizes the use of sources to a detailed implementation of secular intertextual principles.[5] The persistent problem for biblical intertextuality remains even today: no standard or agreed-upon method exists for doing such studies. In effect, intertextuality has become an interdisciplinary approach to the biblical text that often yields varied results depending on the critical approach employed.

Therefore, the following fundamental question must be asked: Is there a way forward for biblical intertextual studies that can resolve the problem

---

4. Fewell, *Reading between Texts*, 17.

5. An example of the former approach is Hatina, "Intertextuality," 28–43. Hatina sees no fruitful relationship between historical-critical studies and intertextual theory. The latter approach was pioneered by Richard Hays in his study of literary echoes in the Pauline Epistles (*Echoes of Scripture*). His method was based on John Hollander's concept of *metalepsis*. Hays defined the latter term as "when the literary echo links the text in which it occurs to an earlier text, the figurative effect of the echo can lie in the unstated or suppressed (transumed) points of resonance between the two texts" (20).

Defending Hope

of methodological inconsistency? Recently, Stefan Alkier proposed that a semiotic approach can serve as the methodological framework for biblical intertextuality and that this type of approach can provide an affirmative response to the question.[6] The purpose for this study, then, is to explore the use of semiotics as an overarching method for doing biblical intertextual studies. The test case for the study will be the Epistle of 1 Peter, a document that exhibits a high saturation of references to the OT.[7] Specifically, I will investigate how a semiotic approach to intertextuality informs an understanding of the relationship between Isaiah and 1 Peter. While other OT books certainly are incorporated into the epistle, at least half of the explicit citations in 1 Peter are from the book of Isaiah. If the implicit references are included, then the total number of Isaianic references increases significantly. Thus, examining only the references to Isaiah will allow for a deeper investigation into the author's primary source. My hope is that such an approach will assist both in locating the intertextual references and in determining their specific function within the framework of Peter's epistle. Additionally, a semiotic approach might also help in determining how the Isaianic references function corporately in the author's presentation of a message of hope and consolation.[8]

Several key terms need to be defined before initiating the investigation. As stated above, *intertextuality* is the dialogue between two or more independent texts, where a *text* is a verbal sign complex.[9] Intertextual studies commonly make use of three terms for identifying references to other texts: *quotation* (or *citation*), *allusion*, and *echo*. A helpful way of viewing these terms is by visualizing them on a spectrum with one side representing

---

6. See Alkier, "Intertextuality," 3–21; and "New Testament Studies," 223–48. In the latter article Alkier presented his all-encompassing semiotic methodology, which can serve as a blueprint for all NT studies, including intertextual investigation. In the former article he examined theoretical aspects of secular intertextuality and delineated how biblical texts would fit into a semiotic framework.

7. Moyise, *Isaiah in the New Testament*, 175, stated, "for the size of the book, 1 Peter ranks alongside Romans and Hebrews for the frequency of its explicit Old Testament quotations."

8. The assumptions made for this study include: (1) texts relate to and are dependent on other texts in some way; (2) the author of 1 Peter chose his references to the OT carefully and for specific purposes; (3) the book of Isaiah is the major source used by the author of 1 Peter and, thus, is crucial to the rhetoric and composition of 1 Peter; and (4) the Epistle of 1 Peter is a unified literary document.

9. The concept of a *text* (and *textuality*) and its relation to a semiotic methodology is examined in greater detail in chapter 2.

Introduction

explicitness and the other side representing implicitness. The most explicit would be a quotation, which is an explicit reference to another text that can be identified by either an introductory formula or verbatim (or near verbatim) linguistic reproduction. An allusion is a less precise, implicit reference to a text that contains at least some commonalities with the referent text. Allusions float somewhere in the middle of the terminology spectrum. Finally, an echo is a vague, distant reference to a text, story, or event by use of similar concepts or thoughts that may or may not have any linguistic commonalities with the referent text. Two other aspects of these definitions include the author's intent in referring to a text and the reader's ability to perceive the intertextual reference. Intent and perception are highest on the explicit side of the spectrum and lowest on the implicit side.

In addition, three terms relating to the methodology need to be defined. A *sign* is something that stands for something other than itself. Signs have no intrinsic meaning but convey meaning within a communicative context. *Semiosis* refers to the actual process of meaning making or sign creation in which a sign, object, and interpretant interact. *Semiotics*, in contrast to semiosis, is a broader term referring to the scientific study of signs and sign systems. Semiotics is not a method but a formal theory of signs and signifying practices. All three terms will be explored in greater depth throughout the book.

Since the method proposed in this book is fairly recent, the foundation for examining 1 Peter must be established in regards to semiotics and intertextual research. Chapters 1 and 2 provide this foundation. In chapter 1, a brief historical sketch of the development of semiotics is provided along with a history of research examining how biblical studies has employed both semiotics and intertextuality. Chapter 2 details the philosophical background of the semiotic method and provides the steps that will be followed for examining the use of Isaiah in 1 Peter. Special attention is given to the thought and works of Charles Sanders Peirce and Umberto Eco, since the semiotic method is based primarily on their work.

Chapters 3–5 are devoted exclusively to a semiotic analysis of 1 Peter. Chapter 3 examines the textual universe (or universe of discourse) of the epistle to determine what assumptions the text makes about reality. In doing so, this analysis sets up the logical world in which the textual signs can both exist and operate. In chapter 4, the encyclopedia of 1 Peter is opened by providing a brief discussion on some of the primary historical and cultural concerns that are imperative for examining the Isaianic references.

Defending Hope

Finally, chapter 5 contains an examination of all the references to Isaiah located in 1 Peter. An analysis of these "signs" proves significant for how and why Peter utilizes this important prophetic work. Moreover, it might well be that Peter is exemplifying, for his suffering audience, what he means in 3:15 when he encourages them to always be ready to give a defense for the hope they have.

1

Semiotics and Biblical Interpretation

IN ORDER TO UNDERSTAND the semiotic method used for this intertextual investigation, a comprehension of the landscape of both semiotics and biblical interpretation is necessary. The chapter begins with a brief historical survey of semiotics from the genesis of the term to its modern-day applications. The inclusion of this section is imperative since the method employed for this study is rooted in semiotic history, especially in the semiotic development of Charles Sanders Peirce (though Peirce is only introduced here since a fuller treatment of his work on semiotics is supplied in chapter 2). Moreover, secular intertextual theorists commonly speak of intertextuality using semiotic language. Next, the major research areas that are germane to this study are surveyed. The pertinent areas of research include intertextuality, biblical studies and semiotics, and 1 Peter and intertextuality. Each research area is treated in turn and focuses on seminal figures and foundational concepts. The aim of this chapter is to provide the theoretical framework for the presentation of the method in chapter 2.

A History of Semiotics[1]

The term *semiotics* derives from the Greek *semeion* (σημεῖον) meaning "sign" and its cognate *semeiotikos* meaning "observant of signs." *Semiotics*

---

1. The following are excellent introductions to the history and development of semiotics: Chandler, *Semiotics: The Basics*; Clarke, *Principles of Semiotic*; Cobley and Jansz, *Introducing Semiotics*; Culler, *The Pursuit of Signs*; Danesi, *The Quest for Meaning*; Hawkes, *Structuralism and Semiotics*; and Nöth, *Handbook of Semiotics*.

was coined by Hippocrates (*ca.* 460–370 B.C.), the founder of Western medicine, as the study of the human body's warning signs, referred to today as symptoms. He believed the *semeion* was the physical form a symptom took and that it pointed to something invisible, such as a specific disease in the body. From this symptomatic identification it is argued that "Hippocrates established medicine as a diagnostic 'semeiotic' science—that is, a science based on the detection and interpretation of bodily signs."[2] For this period in time, the paradigm sign was the medical symptom.

The contribution of Plato (*ca.* 427–347 B.C.) to semiotics is his distinction between natural (or physical) signs and conventional (or man-made) signs. Contrasted with natural signs such as smoke as a sign of fire, conventional signs were those man-made constructs such as words and symbols. For Plato, a significant point was that a word could signify not only an object, but numerous objects that resemble one another. For example, the word *circle* does not refer to merely a single object, but anything with the property of *circularity*.[3] He suggested that the words humans use mirror the mental processes involved in encoding ideas with words. Plato's viewpoint often is referred to as the *mentalist* theory.

Aristotle (384–322 B.C.), a pupil of Plato, differed from his teacher by claiming that words were not properties, but a means for naming objects. His definition of *sign* can be summarized as follows: "(1) Written marks are symbols of spoken sounds. (2) Spoken sounds are (in the first place) signs and symbols of mental impressions. (3) Mental impressions are likenesses of actual things. (4) While mental events and things are the same for all mankind, speech is not."[4] Contrasted with Plato's mentalist theory, Aristotle's is known as the *empirical* theory of signs.

One of the more important discussions on signs in the classical period was that between the Stoics and Epicureans (both *ca.* the early third century B.C.) on the status of the sign. The Stoics believed that natural and conventional signs were related in the sense that they both revealed something intrinsic. Also, the Stoics viewed signs as standing for a proposition or *lekton* (an "intelligible"), which itself described an observable fact. According to this understanding, the *lekton* was part of an inference, the form of which was called *modus ponens*. Essentially, the Stoics understood signs

---

2. Danesi, *The Quest for Meaning*, 6.
3. Ibid.
4. Nöth, *Handbook of Semiotics*, 15.

as one premise of a logical syllogism.⁵ The Epicureans, on the other hand, discounted the inferential theory of the Stoics and held that a sign is not a proposition, but something that can be observed directly. Thus, "it is the observed smoke that is the sign of fire, not the proposition expressed by the sentence 'There is smoke over there.'"⁶

From the viewpoints of these two philosophical groups, a fundamental question arose: Who can interpret a sign? Both Stoics and Epicureans would say that anyone can interpret a sign. However, the Stoics would add that only individuals schooled in formal logic could do so on the basis of inferential theory because their understanding of signs was limited to propositions. Since the Epicureans understood signs as the actual observed reality—not that of a stated or written proposition—their view persisted as the framework for a general theory of signs, which was inclusive of language.

In none of the discussions on signs in the classical tradition did these philosophers and writers speak of words or sentences as linguistic signs (words, both spoken and written, were thought of as symbols).⁷ This important step in the history of semiotics—the connection made between signs and words—did not occur until the work of Augustine (A.D. 354–430).⁸ He saw a distinctive difference between natural signs (*signa naturalia*) and conventional signs (*signa data*). On this major point he differed from the views of the Stoics. For Augustine natural signs, as products of nature, lack intentionality, whereas conventional signs are a direct result of human intention. According to this view, signs such as medical symptoms are natural, and signs such as words and gestures are conventional. Intentionality refers to the production of the sign for purposes of communication. This basic

---

5. For a more detailed account of the Stoics and semiotics, see Eco, *Semiotics and Philosophy*, 29–33.

6. Clarke, *Principles of Semiotic*, 14.

7. Some have posited that Aristotle—in the opening passage of his *De Interpretatione*—was the first to present words as linguistic signs; however, Umberto Eco is quick to dispel this possibility based on the context of the citation and the logic of the statements. For this example and the surrounding discussion, see both Eco, *Semiotics and Philosophy*, 27; and Clarke, *Principles of Semiotic*, 17–18.

8. Augustine details his theory of signs extensively in *De doctrina christiana*. Other works—such as *Confessions*, *De Trinitate*, and *De magistro*—mention signs and communication, but not to the extent that *De doctrina Christiana* does. An extremely helpful and invaluable resource in analyzing Augustine's sign theory is R. A. Markus' *Signs and Meanings* (see especially chapter 4, 105–24).

conception of signs was so significant that it shifted the classical paradigm sign from the medical sign/symptom to the linguistic expression.

The influence Augustine's definition of a sign had upon the development of semiotics in the Western world was significant. His definition proved to be the foundation for most of the work on semiotics that would come in the following millennium. As Deely related, "Augustine defined a sign as 'something that, besides the impressions it conveys to sense, makes something else come into cognition.' Translating more freely, we can say that Augustine defines the sign as anything that, on being perceived brings something besides itself into awareness."[9] Augustine's understanding of the sign is the fundamental understanding from which other theories and definitions derived. In viewing the sign as a sensed particular that points to something not sensed, Augustine is in agreement with the Epicureans. After the death of Augustine, interest in connecting sign production with human understanding waned; but it was revived in the eleventh century.[10] A renewed interest in the classical writers led to the Scholastic movement. The Scholastics used Aristotle's empiricist approach and argued that conventional signs represented practical truths that were not constructed out of convenience—also referred to as the *realist* position.[11] On the other hand, the nominalists claimed that since truth is subjective, signs represent variable human expressions of truth.[12]

John Poinsot (1589–1644) stands out as one of the most influential Renaissance figures in the history of semiotics. In his *Treatise on Signs* (1632), Poinsot systematically examined the issues of unity and scope with regard to the doctrine of signs. He defined the sign as an *intermediary* between things and thoughts that allows the mind to link these intermediary forms with realities in life.[13] As a result, the realities can be

---

9. Deely, "Toward the Origin," 5. Augustine's definitions are located in *Doctr. chr.* I.2.2; II.1.1.

10. Danesi, *The Quest for Meaning*, 7.

11. A noted proponent of the realist view was Thomas Aquinas (1225–1274). Aquinas believed that signs referred to real, actual things even if human variation was part of the process. For more on the Thomist tradition, see Eco and Marmo, eds., *Medieval Theory*, 81–105; and Bains, *The Primacy of Semiosis*, 51–57.

12. Notable nominalists were John Duns Scotus (*ca.* 1266–1308) and William of Ockham (*ca.* 1285–1349). Ockham is significant in that he determined a second type of natural sign, that of Augustine's mental word; that is, the mental conception can now signify in the natural sense.

13. Danesi, *The Quest for Meaning*, 9.

Semiotics and Biblical Interpretation

observed and studied in the forms created to express or signify them. In the age of rationalism, John Locke (1632–1704) is noted for coining the word *semiotics* to refer to a doctrine of signs. He viewed semiotics as an instrument philosophers could use, even going so far as to suggest a plan for formal sign study as a branch of philosophy. His proposition was suggested publicly in the closing paragraphs of his 1690 publication entitled *Essay concerning Human Understanding*. Locke understood two kinds of signs: words and ideas. In his reasoning, words are signs of ideas and ideas are signs: "Locke thus interpreted words as signs of signs, i.e., *metasigns*."[14] As will be addressed below, Locke's separation of words and ideas was challenged by Ferdinand de Sausurre.

The period from Augustine to Locke produced a variety of understandings with regard to both natural and conventional signs. In addition to the classical evidential signs of the Greeks, there were added mental conceptions, mirror images, and sensations. A paradigm shift occurred in which the paradigm sign moved from the medical symptom to spoken and written words. However, "as the variety of natural signs increased, it became increasingly difficult to find common features that warranted applying the same term 'sign' to both these and the signs used in human communication."[15] This major issue was addressed by two key individuals, Ferdinand de Saussure and Charles Sanders Peirce.

In the century that spanned the mid-nineteenth century to the mid-twentieth century, Saussure and Peirce rose as prominent figures in the history of semiotics. Saussure (1857–1913), a Swiss linguist, was the first to propose the term *sémiologie* (*semiology* in English), a science of signs. His perspective on semiology largely has been transferred through notes taken by his students during his lectures. In fact, the first published presentation of Saussure's understanding of signs was provided by his students after his death in a textbook entitled *Cours de linguistique générale* (1916). Though the latter was the first printed evidence of Sausurre's view, he had used the term *sémiologie* at least since 1894. According to Culler, Saussure doubted the foundations upon which contemporary linguistics was practiced, so he argued that "since language was a system of signs linguistics ought to be part of a larger science of signs."[16] Thus, contra Locke, Saussure believed semiotics should not be subsumed under philosophy as a branch of study,

---

14. Nöth, *Handbook of Semiotics*, 24.
15. Clarke, *Principles of Semiotic*, 24–25.
16. Culler, *The Pursuit of Signs*, 22.

but should be an autonomous discipline in and of itself under which other disciplines—like linguistics—should be placed.

Saussure had a precise understanding of the focus of semiology, as the following citation indicates:

> It is possible to conceive of a science which studies the role of signs as part of social life. It would form part of social psychology, and hence of general psychology. We shall call it *semiology* (from the Greek *semeion*, "sign"). It would investigate the nature of signs and the laws governing them. Since it does not yet exist, one cannot say for certain that it will exist. But it has a right to exist, a place ready for it in advance. Linguistics is only one branch of this general science.[17]

The citation demonstrates Saussure's emphasis on the social function of signs. He understood signs as all the devices used in human communication, both linguistic and non-linguistic. Another point of significance gleaned from his writings is his proposition that language should be studied not only based on its individual parts, but also based on the relationships among these parts.[18] On this point, Saussure stated that a linguistic sign was composed of two parts that, like a sheet of paper, were of the same entity: the signified (concept) and the signifier (sound-image). In summary, Saussure is not only remembered for his groundbreaking work on signs, but is also considered the founder of modern linguistics. His work eventually influenced the later development of structuralism.

The second individual during this time period was American philosopher C. S. Peirce (1839–1914). Peirce brought Locke's term *semiotics* into wide circulation and, along with Saussure, is viewed as the cofounder of modern semiotics. According to Danesi, the greatest insight afforded by Peirce was that "our sensory and emotional experience of the world influences how a sign is constituted and why it has been brought into existence in the first place."[19] At the time of Peirce's work, he was ignored largely by his contemporaries, but today he is regarded as one of the most influential individuals in the long history of semiotics.

---

17. See Bally and Sechehaye, from the translation of *Cours de linguistique générale* by W. Baskin, *Course in General Linguistics*, 15–16.

18. For a technical discussion of Saussure at this point, see Hawkes, *Structuralism and Semiotics*, 8–16.

19. Danesi, *The Quest for Meaning*, 10.

Peirce's approach was different than Saussure in that he attempted to develop an autonomous semiotics that was not subordinate or superordinate to any other discipline. Indeed, Peirce devoted his whole life and work to semiotics because his basic conviction was that signs were present everywhere. The following citation from Peirce in the context of a discussion on issues of pragmaticism reveals his conviction as to the pervasiveness of signs:

> It seems a strange thing, when one comes to ponder over it, that a sign should leave its interpreter to supply a part of its meaning; but the explanation of the phenomenon lies in the fact that the entire universe—not merely the universe of existents, but all that wider universe, embracing the universe of existents as a part, the universe which we are all accustomed to refer to as "the truth"— that all this universe is perfused with signs, if it is not composed exclusively of signs.[20]

Here Peirce made his stance on signs most explicit: they are what the universe is composed of and they require interpreters to complete their meaning. Based on a proliferation of signs, he argued that semiotics would be the science of sciences.

Peirce defined a *sign* (also called *representamen*) as "something which stands to somebody for something in some respect or capacity."[21] A sign stands for something, which he referred to as its *object*. Further, a sign creates in the mind of the person an equivalent idea or sign, which he labeled the *interpretant*. According to Peirce, the three elements of sign, object, and interpretant formed the triadic sign relation. Thus, Peirce further developed Saussure's two components of signifier and signified into a triadic unit. The triad was a direct reflection of Peirce's revision of Immanuel Kant's universal categories. Peirce narrowed Kant's twelve categories down to three: firstness, secondness, and thirdness.[22] Each category correlated to one aspect of the sign triad: sign = firstness, object = secondness, and interpretant = thirdness. In his entire approach to signs and sign relations, Peirce aimed at universality regarding epistemology. Much of the subsequent work in semiotics is rooted in either Peirce or Saussure.

---

20. Hartshorne and Weiss, *Collected Papers*, 302. All subsequent references to Peirce's works will be from this edited series, unless otherwise stated, and will follow the abbreviated format for citation (CP vol:page).

21. CP 2:228.

22. CP 8:328.

Defending Hope

Semiotic work after Peirce largely moved in one of two directions, typically according to geographical location. In the United States, semiotics followed the work of Peirce, but ventured into the realm of the emerging science of comparative animal psychology.[23] In continental Europe, work continued along the lines of semiology (Saussure) and had an anthropocentric tendency.[24] Modern semioticians employ findings from related disciplines such as linguistics, philosophy, anthropology, and psychology. Thus, semiotics is viewed by most practitioners as an interdisciplinary approach.[25]

A Survey of Selected Research Areas

The first research area addressed below is that of intertextuality. Both the secular and biblical contexts of this field of study are examined in turn. An intriguing realm of study involves how biblical scholars have employed semiotics in an analysis of the biblical text (and not necessarily biblical intertextuality). The second subsection outlines this research area. Finally, the third subsection provides a survey of the intertextual work done in 1 Peter. This final section narrows the survey of research to the test case of this study, highlighting specifically whether any work has been done on Isaiah in 1 Peter and semiotics in 1 Peter.

---

23. Notables here are Charles Morris (who distinguished three dimensions of semiotics: syntactics, semantics, and pragmatics) and Thomas Sebeok (who pioneered work in biological semiotics or zoosemiotics).

24. Notables here include Roland Barthes and Umberto Eco. One cannot overstate the significance of Eco for modern-day semiotic advances. According to Danesi, "it was Eco who single-handedly put semiotics on the map of pop culture with his best-selling novel *The Name of the Rose*" (*The Quest for Meaning*, 11). Moreover, he has argued cogently for semiotics as a science (see his list of five fundamentals in Danesi, *The Quest for Meaning*, 24).

25. Eco, *A Theory of Semiotics*, 9–14 lists the following as disciplines which belong to the semiotic field: zoosemiotics, olfactory signs, tactile communication, codes of taste, paralinguistics, medical semiotics, kinesics and proxemics, musical codes, formalized languages, written languages/unknown alphabets/secret codes, natural languages, visual communication, systems of objects, plot structure, text theory, cultural codes, aesthetic texts, mass communication, and rhetoric.

Intertextuality

Since intertextuality was introduced as such in secular literary studies, a brief history of the term and its application within this sphere is provided. Theoretical and foundational issues are emphasized, especially where these issues highlight the semiotic origins of intertextuality. The second subsection is an examination of intertextuality in the sphere of biblical studies. Emphasis here is on theory, major interpretive issues, and methodological approaches.

Secular Intertextuality

As noted in the previous section, Julia Kristeva coined *intertextuality*. The context for the genesis of her intertextual theory was in 1960s Paris during the heyday of Sausurrean structuralism. Her reason for going to Paris was to study literary theory under Roland Barthes, one of the most famous proponents of poststructuralism. In many ways the work of Barthes and Kristeva was a microcosm of the transitional period in literary theory, which can be described as a shift from structuralism to poststructuralism. Graham Allen described this shift: "If structuralist literary critics believe that Saussurean linguistics can help criticism become objective, even scientific in nature, then poststructuralist critics of the 1960s and beyond have argued that criticism, like literature itself, is inherently unstable, the product of subjective desires and drives."[26] The work of both Kristeva and Barthes is rooted in a poststructuralist approach to literature.

In addition to a Saussurean linguistic and structuralist background, Kristeva also was influenced heavily by the Russian literary theorist Mikhail Bakhtin. Of particular significance were the sociopolitical situations of France (Barthes and Kristeva) and Russia (Bakhtin).[27] Both contexts were experiencing political and social crises. In 1960s France, revolutionary events such as student and worker uprisings threatened the authority of the French government. In 1960s and 1970s Russia, previous Stalin censorship of literary theory was fading and, as a result, this context allowed for a rediscovery of Bakhtin's work. The following is a survey of the views of

---

26. Allen, *Intertextuality*, 3.

27. The following comments in this paragraph are summarized from Allen, *Intertextuality*, 16.

Defending Hope

Kristeva, Barthes, and Bakhtin and their impact upon intertextual theory. Three of their noted successors are discussed briefly as well.

In her 1974 dissertation, Kristeva explored intertextual theory as the relationship between the semiotic (drives and dispositions of the prelinguistic phase) and the symbolic (positioning of the subject in a symbolic order).[28] Her exploration is evidenced in her definition of intertextuality as the transposition of sign systems into one another. Kristeva argued that since texts are so dependent on one another, they can have no autonomy or univocality. She concluded that texts are polyvocal and then defined the intertextual enterprise as an "intersection of textual surfaces rather than a fixed point (a fixed meaning)."[29] For Kristeva, however, texts were not merely poetic or secular literary works, but culture as a whole was a text. Thus, her intertextual theory involved both literary criticism and a semiotics of culture; a text no longer could be referenced apart from the entire universe of texts. She borrowed the concept of dialogism from Bakhtin (discussed below) and resolved that all texts are in discourse together.

Before structuralism dominated literary theory, the author of a text was considered as the source of meaning in a work. Such a view was referred to as *influence*.[30] Theories of influence were characterized by context, tradition, and the agency of the author. The rise of French structuralism, however, sparked a shift toward a rejection of the author in favor of the view that texts absorb one another; thus, meaning is elusive. Kristeva adopted this understanding and posited that both author and reader disappear due to the anonymity of the general text.[31] Additionally, her approach was almost entirely philosophical and did not allow for textual analysis. Finally, a significant matter bearing upon this present investigation is that Kristeva was not interested in any methodological implications of her intertextual theory. In fact, her definition of intertextuality as a *transposition* of sign systems evidenced her intentional disciplinary limiting of the concept. For this reason, many who followed her sought to mine out a methodology from her intertextual theory.

---

28. See Kristeva, *Revolution in Poetic Language*.

29. Kristeva, *Desire in Language*, 65.

30. For a discussion of the major differences between influence and intertextuality in literary theory, see Clayton and Rothstein, *Influence and Intertextuality*, 3–31.

31. Alkier refers to Kristeva's move toward a plurality of ways in thought and life as "the slipping of meaning" ("Intertextuality," 5).

Like Kristeva, Barthes's conception of intertextual theory was grounded in Sausurrean semiology.[32] He claimed that a text does not produce a single theological meaning, but creates an environment where words and thoughts can blend and clash. Both his understanding of a text and the work of a textual critic were contrary to the traditional formulations of *text* and *work*. Barthes is known perhaps most for his view of the author in intertextual theory. In his essay entitled "The Death of the Author," he argued that the figure of an author was a modern, capitalist creation that conveniently attached a name to a work.[33] Barthes understood a *work* as promoting a form of interpretation whereby the interrelation between author, work, and reader defined reading as a form of consumption. Thus, for him the author (or the author's name) points to a *work*, which contrasts with a *text*.[34] The emphasis for Barthes was in the realm of *text*. Barthes also developed five *codes* to determine the intertextuality of a particular reading (which function as a sort of methodology).[35]

The most influential figure for Kristeva's notion of intertextuality, however, was the Russian postformalist Mikhail Bakhtin. In his critique of formalism, Bakhtin proposed the notion of *dialogism*, which he defined as an open-ended conversation between the text, addressee, and culture.[36] Bakhtin never formulated a theory of intertextuality, but rather focused on all utterances as having a dialogic characteristic. Bakhtin proposed that *dialogism* was a constitutive element of both language and literature. According to his view, every word has dialogic quality; that is, "every word is directed toward an *answer* and cannot escape the profound influence of the answering word that it anticipates."[37] From his dialogic theory he argued that a linguistic sign cannot be analyzed in isolation, but only in relation to other signs.

32. See his *Elements of Semiology*.

33. Barthes, "The Death," 142–48.

34. Ibid., 143.

35. Barthes's discussion of these codes is found in *S/Z*. The five codes are as follows: the hermeneutic code concerns textual elements that force the reader to interpret events; the code of the seme concerns the connotative quality associated with an action or character; the symbolic code includes all symbolic patterns; the proairetic code concerns the actions present in the narrative; and finally, the cultural code involves the knowledge or wisdom referred to in the text that relates directly to cultural authorities and communal thinking.

36. Bakhtin, *Rabelais and His World*; ibid., *Problems of Dostoevsky's Poetics*.

37. Bakhtin, *The Dialogic Imagination*, 280. He worked with two main concepts within his formulation of dialogism: *heteroglossia* (other-languagedness) and *polyphony* (many-voicedness). Heteroglossia describes language as an intersection of many languages

Defending Hope

In sum, for Bakhtin language is an open system and one that exhibits diversity in dialogue. The dependence of Kristeva's work on Bakhtin is exhibited most clearly in her application of dialogism to the entire universe of texts and her formulation of intertextuality on the basis of sign systems. The major contrast between her and Bakhtin, however, is that the latter maintained that dialogicality could exist only as a quality of words or utterances. Kristeva, in her definitional statement of intertextuality, expanded Bakhtin's concept by applying dialogicality not only to words but to texts as well.

Following Kristeva's groundbreaking work, poststructural theorists utilized intertextual theory to impede beliefs of consistent or stable meaning and objective interpretations. One such theorist who stands out on this account is Jacques Derrida. Derrida was a French philosopher and literary critic—best known for his work on the theory of deconstructionism—who believed that intertextuality was a limitless deferral from one text to another. Resulting from this deferral is the view that a text is never a finished work but constantly is being revised by what comes after it.[38] Currently, poststructuralist critiques of author and influence are still adhered to, while only rarely some concession is given to the agency of the author.

Michael Riffaterre stands out as a successor of Kristeva who actually delimited the scope of intertextual theory. On the one hand, he placed much emphasis on the reader and on textual semiotics while, on the other hand, his theory insists "on a determinate conception of the literary artifact, one that rejects the dispersal of meanings through an infinite system of interlocking codes."[39] For Riffaterre, intertextuality can operate as a "constraint upon reading," which restricts the reader's freedom and guides the reader's interpretation of a text.[40] He argued that a valid interpretation can be based only in a stable picture of the text. Such stability is achieved by the reader's repeated perception of *constants*, and from these constants the reader can determine

---

in many different ways. Polyphony (in reference to a literary novel) refers to the voices of author, reader, and characters and how these distinct, yet equal, voices in a text interact and shape one another.

38. Derrida, "Living On: Border Lines."

39. Clayton and Rothstein, *Influence and Intertextuality*, 24.

40. Riffaterre, "Syllepsis," 628. In this intriguing article on intertextuality, Riffaterre demonstrated Derrida's concept of *syllepsis* by examining some of the latter's selected works. Riffaterre defined syllepsis as "a word understood in two different ways at once, as meaning and as significance" (638). He argued that syllepsis sums up a text's duality—its semantic and semiotic units—and thus should be understood as the literary sign *par excellence*.

the proper interpretation of a text. Moreoever, Riffaterre's dependence on semiotics is evident in his description of the primary obstacle to interpretation: an incomplete reading.[41] In essence, Riffaterre argued for the restrictive nature of intertextuality, a position that simultaneously distances him from the plurality that characterizes Kristeva, Barthes, and Derrida.

A final aspect that necessitates brief mention is the primary weakness of secular intertextual theory. Jonathan Culler, a prolific writer on semiotics, linguistics, and intertextual theory, has issued a critique of poststructuralist forms of intertextuality in which he pointed out the major issue that has plagued all applications of this theory: they are contradictory in nature.[42] He asserted that an application of intertextual theory to specific readings naturally reduces and restricts intertextuality to something contrary to what it is claimed to be. Culler highlighted the tension between the historical and the theoretical when approaching intertextual study.[43] This tension exists as well in the history of biblical intertextuality and its applications. To this the discussion now turns.

Biblical Intertextuality

In the realm of biblical studies, intimations of intertextuality—or the use of the OT in the NT—can be found in studies on the sources the NT writers utilized in constructing their documents. One of the first individuals to propose an intertextual paradigm was C. H. Dodd.[44] He posited that the use of the OT by the writers of the NT reveals the substructure of NT theology. A crucial conclusion reached by Dodd was that the NT writers quoted particular verses of the OT not as individual testimonies in themselves, but as pointers to the surrounding OT context. Thus, the OT was the primary source (or substructure) for the theology of the NT. In the decade following

---

41. For his discussion on interpretation, stability, and constants, see Riffaterre, "Interpretation and Undecidability," 227–42. On the semiotic foundation of his interpretation of texts, he states that "an incomplete reading . . . can have only two causes: failure to recognize a verbal sign for what it is and/or improper identification of its referent" (227).

42. See Culler, *The Pursuit of Signs*, 100–118.

43. Like Riffaterre, Culler argued for the constraining power of intertextuality with his concept of *conventions*. Conventions serve to restrict endless signification. As Culler stated, "Because literary works do have meaning for readers, semiotics undertakes to describe the systems of convention responsible for those meanings" (*The Pursuit of Signs*, 38–39).

44. Dodd, *According to the Scriptures*.

Dodd, Barnabas Lindars expounded upon Dodd's thesis, claiming that the NT writers used the OT to illustrate the great doctrinal truths of Scripture.[45]

In the last half of the twentieth century, numerous articles and monographs on issues pertaining to intertextuality surfaced. As intertextuality became a growing interest for biblical scholars, some noticed that a major part of this study was determining the exegetical methods of the NT authors in using the OT. A second and related issue was whether their methods were descriptive or normative for modern-day interpreters. In 1975, Richard Longenecker was at the forefront of this particular aspect of biblical intertextuality.[46] He outlined the Jewish exegetical procedures during the apostolic period, describing methods such as *peshat* (literal), *pesher*, *midrash*, and allegory. After examining the NT writings and their implementation of these methods, Longenecker surmised that while the conclusions of the NT writers should be adopted, one should not seek to reproduce their exegetical methods.

One of the most influential and important figures in the past twenty-five years of biblical intertextual research was Richard Hays. Arguably, Hays's monograph entitled *Echoes of Scripture in the Letters of Paul* changed the landscape of biblical intertextual study by tying it to the secular literary theories of textuality and intertextuality. In this work, Hays applied intertextual theory to an examination of Paul's citations and allusions to specific texts of the OT. He provided a concise summary of the work of literary critics on the role of tradition in literature, particularly the works of T. S. Eliot and Harold Bloom. However, John Hollander's *The Figure of Echo: A Mode of Allusion in Milton and After* was very influential in Hays's construction of his method. Utilizing Hollander's conception of literary allusion, Hays proposed that the allusive echo serves as a diachronic trope that links the text to an earlier one to produce a new figuration or signification. He referred to this new figuration as *metalepsis* and defined this term as a process that "places the reader within a field of whispered or unstated correspondences."[47] Hays claimed that *metalepsis* was the method of Paul when echoing OT Scripture.

The significance of Hays's work lies not only in his application of metalepsis to intertextual links but also in his presentation of seven tests

---

45. Lindars, *New Testament Apologetic*.
46. Longenecker, *Biblical Exegesis*.
47. Hays, *Echoes of Scripture*, 20.

Semiotics and Biblical Interpretation

for hearing echoes.[48] These tests were critical in that they proposed a common starting point for scholars in approaching the field of intertextuality. Almost every literature review section of scholarly monographs and dissertations that address intertextuality treats the work of Hays to some degree. While all seven of Hays's tests are not agreed upon universally, his work was significant for issuing a call to those performing intertextual studies to adopt a common methodological approach.

If Hays is noted for his implementation of secular intertextual theory in biblical studies, then Carol Newsom should be mentioned for her application of Bakhtin's dialogism to biblical studies. In one particular article, Newsom provided insights from Bakhtin's concept of dialogic truth and polyphony as they relate to biblical studies.[49] After distinguishing between monologic and dialogic truth, she focused most of her work on an application of the latter concept to whole books of the OT. Newsom defined dialogic truth as a perception about the nature of discourse that conceptualizes truth as the point of intersection of several unmerged voices. Bakhtin believed that polyphonic writing could produce a genuine dialogue by drawing the reader into conversation with ideas. Applying this concept of dialogism to biblical texts respects the variety and particularity of the Bible and keeps readings in their historical contexts. In her work, Newsom demonstrated the significance of Bakhtin's theory and the application of this theory to biblical texts—even if only on a macrolevel.

In contrast to both Hays and Newsom, Thomas Hatina stands out as one who viewed the secular, poststructuralist context of intertextuality—and all the theoretical viewpoints contained therein—as destructive for biblical and textual inquiry. In one particular article, Hatina addressed the use of the term *intertextuality* among biblical scholars as done rather loosely and without regard to some of the key theoretical issues that surrounded the origination of the term.[50] In particular, he asserted that this context is detrimental to historical-critical inquiry. He criticized historical critics for having failed to consider three characteristics of intertextuality: the ideological context, the concept of text, and the distinction between influence and intertextuality. Hatina pointed out several crucial issues that

---

48. Hays's seven tests—which function as methodological steps—are availability, volume, recurrence, thematic coherence, historical plausibility, history of interpretation, and satisfaction (*Echoes of Scripture*, 29–32).

49. Newsom, "Dialogic Truth," 290–306.

50. As argued by Hatina, "Intertextuality," 28–43.

biblical scholars should consider when referring to an intertextual method of study as it pertains to historical inquiry of the biblical texts. In many ways, he challenged biblical scholars to rethink not only the use of the term itself, but also how best one should implement intertextuality into the framework of historical criticism.

At this point in the history of biblical intertextuality, the analogy of a spectrum is helpful for plotting the various viewpoints on intertextual theory and practice. At one end is indebtedness to secular literary theory that approaches intertextuality as an open-ended concept, whereby a determination of meaning can be achieved but often allows for numerous levels of meaning. Moreover, the author's intention for citing the OT is discarded and meaning generally is located in the reader's ability to perceive. At the other end, secular literary theory is abandoned in favor of a strict historical-critical approach that places a great deal of control on a determination of meaning in the text. Emphasis here is on the author's intention and less on the role of the reader. On this issue, George Aichele and Gary Phillips have pleaded with biblical scholars to make a conscious and informed decision on how to employ intertextuality, either as an open-ended, systems-oriented process with little to no boundaries or as an emerging discipline to be used alongside existing critical methodologies.[51]

Perhaps one of the most prolific writers on biblical intertextuality is NT and intertextual scholar Steve Moyise. He has written numerous introductory texts on intertextuality in which he examined both theory and method. In 2001, Moyise produced a basic introductory textbook on the use of the OT in the NT.[52] He related the difference of quoting texts in the modern world to that of the ancient world. Today one must be careful to cite verbatim and in accordance with the larger context; in the ancient world, texts were living traditions that often were interpreted in light of a newer situation.

Moyise also has provided a helpful survey of five major types of intertextuality that are employed by biblical scholars.[53] First, *intertextual echo*—an approach pioneered by Richard Hays—focuses on textual traces that are unconscious and that form the cultural backdrop of Israel's heritage. Second, *narrative intertextuality* can be described as an author's evocation not of a particular text but of a particular story. Third, *exegetical intertextuality* focuses on the exegetical methods of an author and specifically on those

---

51. Aichele and Phillips, "Introduction," 7–18.
52. Moyise, *Old Testament in New*.
53. Moyise, "Intertextuality and Biblical Studies," 418–31.

passages where exegetical activity may not be present in the text. Fourth, *dialogical intertextuality* views intertextual links as a two-way process in which both new and old texts affect each other. Finally, *postmodern intertextuality* emphasizes the subjective element of this type of study by proposing that meaning will never be exhausted through interpretation. The influence of Bakhtin and Kristeva is seen foremost in the latter two types of intertextuality. In summarizing Moyise's stance on intertextuality, he is one who falls in the middle of the spectrum outlined above. He argued that an author may have had a specific intention in referencing Scripture, but that the effects generated from this are out of his control. Thus, he placed equal importance on the author and the reader.

One final individual deserving mention is Stanley Porter. His primary contribution to intertextual studies is he is the leading voice for terminological clarity and methodological consistency.[54] For Porter, these two issues are the major interpretive cruxes of intertextual research. He has argued four main points that scholars must take into account: knowing the goal of the investigation and what should be considered as evidence, defining and rigorously applying categories, combining author- and audience-oriented approaches, and formulating a comprehensive perspective on determining citations. Porter also contended that a method must be developed that takes into account the range of ways in which a text can be utilized, both on micro and macrolevels. Currently, the state of biblical intertextuality is one that is still responding to Porter's challenges. The field is plagued by a multiplicity of approaches and a plethora of terms for determining references to Scripture.

Biblical Studies and Semiotics

The history of semiotics and of intertextuality poses a significant question for biblical studies: If signs are located in linguistics and human communication, then what application does semiotics have to the text of the Bible and, specifically, to biblical intertextuality? Studies that implement a semiotic approach to the biblical text are sparse. The following discussion highlights some of the individuals who apply a semiotic perspective to the biblical text. As will be demonstrated, only a few of these individuals

---

54. The pertinent works of Porter on these two issues are "The Use," 79–96; and "Further Comments," 98–110.

examine the text through a comprehensive semiotic lens, while the others utilize semiotics only minimally.

Susan Wittig exemplified an early attempt at approaching the biblical text through a semiotic lens.[55] In her article for the experimental journal *Semeia*, she examined how a theory of multiple meanings (or plurisignification) is best explained using a semiotic model of analysis. Much of her work in this article is on the explication of a structural-semiotic model indebted primarily to Saussure. She applied the model to a basic reading scenario of the parables of Jesus in their various contexts to demonstrate how one text can be read differently by others. Wittig concluded by incorporating Wolfgang Iser's work on the phenomenology of the reading act into her semiotic model. Thus, Wittig presented her theory of multiple meanings as one attributed to the recognition and interpretation of signs (here, the parabolic sign), the latter of which have their meaning in the context of the reading act.

In 1988, Gordon Whitney presented a paper entitled "A Semiotic Approach to Old Testament Fulfilment Citations in the Fourth Gospel" at the annual meeting of the Evangelical Theological Society.[56] Whitney introduced the paper by describing briefly both semiotics and semiosis. He followed the work of C. S. Peirce by examining selected OT texts in John's Gospel on the basis of the sign triad (sign, object, and interpretant). Whitney's basic argument was that the macrostructure of the Fourth Gospel is presented as a network of signs. He suggested that *sense* is one aspect of a sign, whereas *reference* is one aspect of an object, and from the sign-object interaction he derived the *kind-of-sense* (labeled as either literal or figurative) of each OT citation examined. The interpretants—which are illuminated by asking "leading questions" of the text—bring forth a new interpretation of the citation in the context of the Fourth Gospel, which functions as a higher level of sign.

Whitney's following description of interpretants is significant for semiotics and intertextuality: "An interpretant is to be understood as the specific application in a given triad of some more general theory, interpretive principle, or controlling paradigm. The one giving the sign may make the interpretant explicit but for signs which are verbal rather than visual this is not normal and might make the literature seem unnatural in its style

---

55. Wittig, "A Theory," 75–103.
56. Whitney, "A Semiotic Approach."

and message."⁵⁷ Whitney's definition of interpretant coheres with Peirce's description of an interpretant, which he defined as the idea to which the sign-object relation gives rise and even the further sign that is created through the sign-object relation. The significance of Whitney's work was the presentation of a concise illustration of how semiotics can be applied to the study of the OT in the NT.

Terry Prewitt's approach to a reading of Genesis was based on what he called a *structural-semiotic* approach.⁵⁸ He examined aspects of the book such as the genealogies, polity and history, mythos and ethos, and structural hermeneutics. In the preface he noted the influence of Algirdas Greimas upon his thinking on Genesis. Greimas is noted for developing *narratology*, a branch of semiotics that examines how humans in all cultures invent similar narratives.⁵⁹ Overall, Prewitt's approach was more structural than semiotic, relegating a discussion of the latter to a five-page chapter at the end of the book. However, his comments on semiotics are insightful for intertextual study. Prewitt's basic understanding of semiosis in the context of biblical reading is that each culture (ancient and modern) produces its own interpretation of texts based on their community and context, thus arguing for a potential of meaning. Further, he stated that "the idea of 'cumulative transmission of learning' is central to semiosis, the active process of experience through signs."⁶⁰ Therefore, Prewitt's study merely mentioned semiotics in relation to a theory of interpretation and did not apply the concept as a thorough methodological approach.

In the realm of philosophy and hermeneutics, Anthony C. Thiselton has written extensively on the various hermeneutical paradigms that have been applied to the biblical text. In particular, he has provided a detailed account of the history of semiotics and its significance for issues concerning theories of textuality and the role of the reader in the interpretive process.⁶¹ He addressed a major interpretive question that semiotics poses for biblical hermeneutics: Does semiotic theory necessarily lead to deconstructionism? This question is a valid one since most of the work in twentieth-century semiotic theory was done by poststructuralists and deconstructionists, both

---

57. Ibid., 2.

58. Prewitt, *The Elusive Covenant*.

59. In relation to Greimas and narratology, Danesi commented that, in essence, "narrativity undergirds both conversations and fictional texts" (*The Quest for Meaning*, 107).

60. Prewitt, *The Elusive Covenant*, 130.

61. See especially his articles on semiotics in Thiselton, *New Horizons*.

of whom emphasize the priority of the reader in the interpretive process. Thiselton's proposition was that postmodernist and deconstructionist proponents—such as Barthes and Derrida—push semiotic theory beyond its own limits and, as a result, they clothe their postmodernist worldviews in semiotic language. He also examined the influential figures in the development of secular intertextual theory—such as Bakhtin and Kristeva—and their incorporation of semiotic elements. The overall contribution of Thiselton to a discussion of biblical studies and semiotics is his warning to the interpreter not to get trapped within one particular philosophical tradition when approaching the text. One's ever-present worldview naturally will affect one's interpretation of and approach to the text.

In 1996, Antti Laato applied a semiotic framework and method to a large-scale examination of OT prophetic literature.[62] Based on the conviction that Peircean semiotics can function as a model theory for the study, Laato applied semiotic theory first to a survey of methods of studying OT prophetic literature and second to the interpretation of this literature. Laato's explanation of her choice of Peircean semiotics for her approach to biblical texts is extremely enlightening for the present discussion. Her basic argument is as follows:

> Biblical interpretation is based on the analysis of texts. Therefore we define the process of text writing and reading in terms of Peircean semiotics . . . The writer of a text has some object (historical event, imagination world, a plot in the detective novel etc.) which is vague or indefinite in his mind and which he attempts to communicate. Because it is impossible to communicate an object which is vague in the writer's mind he must clothe it in formulations which his mind can master. This systematic form can be called the *referential world* . . . which is an interpretant of that dynamic object which the writer attempts to present by the sign (= the text).[63]

Here Laato presented a clear and concise way of understanding the relationship of Peirce's sign triad to any given text. The explanation provided by Laato on texts and semiotics can be helpful in ascertaining why an author would cite or allude to a text. Thus, the import of her approach is the application of Peirce's semiotic theory to biblical texts.

---

62. Laato, *History and Ideology*.
63. Ibid., 53.

The recent work by Marko Jauhiainen is included here because his intertextual approach to the use of Zechariah in Revelation incorporates aspects of semiotics.[64] The influence of semiotics can be seen primarily in the definition he adopted for an allusion. In his section on terminology, he stated that he followed Ziva Ben-Porat's definition of a literary allusion, which in essence states that such a device activates two texts simultaneously through the interaction of a sign and a larger referent.[65] According to Ben-Porat, the referent is always an independent text. In addition to Ben-Porat's definition, Jauhiainen also noted that this understanding was close to Michael Thompson's definition of an allusion. Thompson stated that "literary critics concur that allusion involves (1) the use of a sign or marker that (2) calls to the reader's mind another known text (3) for a specific purpose."[66] In a very broad sense, the definitions of Ben-Porat and Thompson—which form the basic stance on allusions taken by Jauhiainen—point to the process of semiosis. While Jauhiainen's study did not mention semiosis or semiotics, his approach leaned heavily in this direction.

Of the individuals surveyed above, all except for Whitney and Laaato implemented a semiotic approach only to the extent that such an approach served as a theory for understanding meaning. A final individual to mention here is Stefan Alkier, who holds the distinction of proposing semiotics as an all-encompassing methodological approach to biblical texts. Recently, Alkier has delineated how a "semiotic doctrine of methodology" is a valid method for NT study and specifically for intertextual studies.[67] His proposition rests on the application of Peirce's three categories of sign, object, and interpretant to linguistic signs (e.g., the biblical text). For this reason, he terms his approach *categorical semiotics*—as opposed to the other two semiotic exegetical approaches of *structuralist semiotics* and *poststructuralist semiotics*.

The question that surfaces at this point is, "Why categorical semiotics?" In response to this question, Alkier articulated six basic convictions for his view on semiotics as the way to approach biblical studies.[68]

64. Jauhiainen, *Zechariah in Revelation*.

65. Ibid., 29. See Ben-Porat, "The Poetics," 107–8.

66. Thompson, *Clothed with Christ*, 29.

67. Alkier outlined his "semiotic doctrine of methodology" in two articles: "Intertextuality," 3–21; and "New Testament Studies," 223–48. The fundamentals of his approach were initially worked out and applied in the following two works by Alkier: *Wunder und Wirklichkeit* and "From Text to Intertext," 1–18.

68. These convictions are summarized from Alkier, "New Testament Studies," 223–24.

First, the object of NT study is the NT itself and its cultural context—this includes aspects of intra-, inter-, and extra-textuality. Second, both the OT and NT are generated by signs; thus, studying the NT involves studying sign production and reception. Third, the cultures of the NT world must be examined in their respective encyclopedias, an area that semiotics addresses.[69] Fourth, categorical semiotics provides biblical studies with a common theoretical basis and promotes interdisciplinary approaches. Fifth, such an approach promotes a pluralistic community of interpretation. Sixth, "the categorical semiotics of Charles Sanders Peirce provides the necessary and sufficient formal categories to comprehend rightly what the object of biblical studies is—namely, the biblical texts, which are written signs—and to examine fully and critically the diversity of their relationships and the multifarious effects of meaning that result from them."[70] After stating these convictions, Alkier launched into a systematic presentation of his semiotic methodology for NT study. Since his method will be followed for this study, a detailed description of his work will be included in the Methodology section below.

1 Peter and Intertextuality

In 1976, John H. Elliott diagnosed the status of 1 Peter as "second-class" and "one of the stepchildren of the NT canon" due to the neglect of this epistle by NT scholars.[71] Following his strong critique of the academic guild, a boom in studies on 1 Peter came that examined various aspects of this epistle. Nearly a quarter of a century after his initial diagnosis, Elliott commented positively on this change in status in his magisterial commentary on 1 Peter.[72] Of the studies that have appeared over the last thirty years or so, some have focused specifically on textual and exegetical issues involved in an intertextual analysis of OT citations and allusions. In this final section of the literature review, the major figures involved in intertextual research in 1 Peter are treated. The discussion will focus on the application of their studies and the methods they employ.

---

69. The term *encyclopedia* is a term introduced by Peirce and understood by Alkier to refer to the world of the text. This term is explored in chapter 2.

70. Alkier, "New Testament Studies," 224.

71. Elliott, "The Rehabilitation," 243–54.

72. Elliott, *1 Peter*, 6.

In his 1968 dissertation, Thomas Lea examined the OT references in 1 Peter.[73] Although intertextual work in 1 Peter had been done in periodicals and essays, Lea's work was the first full-length treatment of the use of the OT in 1 Peter. He examined the OT in the Petrine literature—including Peter's speeches in Acts—through a historical-critical lens and concluded that 1 Peter used the OT typologically to create OT applications to Peter's life situation and to communicate that the life of Jesus was the fulfillment of the visions of the OT prophets. A main criticism of Lea's work was that he did not recognize any overarching theme that explains the use of the OT in 1 Peter. W. Edward Glenny supplemented Lea's work by adding a hermeneutical interest to a systematic investigation of the OT in 1 Peter.[74] Glenny specifically focused on methods of interpretation by the author of 1 Peter and came up with nine hermeneutical classifications: literal use, typological-prophetic use, analogy, illustration, legal proof, proof passage, exemplary use, direct prophecy, and midrash. The two most common classifications he discovered were typological-prophetic and analogy.

Two years later, Dan McCartney further nuanced Glenny's work by arguing that the contrast between exegetical methods of 1 Peter and other Jewish exegetical methods differed only in regard to hermeneutical goal.[75] He concluded that the hermeneutic of 1 Peter should be paradigmatic for any Christian interpretation. William Schutter aimed to clarify the hermeneutical presuppositions and methods of the author's use of the OT in 1 Peter.[76] He focused primarily on literary aspects of the epistle and the placement of the OT in this structure. Schutter's contributions lie in the areas of OT quotation analysis and thematic analysis (he concluded that *suffering* was the overarching theme of the epistle).

In a 2002 article, Steve Moyise and Fika van Rensburg combined aspects of intertextuality with historical, grammatical, and structural modes of interpretation to explore the textual dynamics of 1 Pet 3:13–17.[77] Their aim was to demonstrate how both traditional methods of interpretation and recent literary theory are imperative for interpreting a text. Through a preliminary survey of Isaianic texts in 1 Peter, Moyise and van Rensburg

---

73. Lea, "Peter's Use."

74. Glenny, "The Hermeneutics."

75. McCartney, "First Epistle of Peter."

76. Schutter, *Hermeneutic and Composition*.

77. van Rensburg and Moyise, "1 Peter 3:13–17," 275–86. See also their similar approach in "1 Peter 2:4–10," 12–30.

concluded that the author of 1 Peter rarely strayed from the most common Isaiah texts used in Christian tradition. Additionally, they argued that the author had at least two Isaianic texts in mind, and this would point to the quotation as introducing a second source of meaning. In sum, Moyise and van Rensburg demonstrated how intertextuality can point to the ongoing effects of meaning—many times unintended by the author—that echoes can generate. In that same year, Mark Dubis examined the motif of the *messianic woes* found particularly in 1 Pet 4:12–19.[78] He claimed that these woes fit into the larger exile-restoration motif of the book in that the hopes for restoration claimed in Isa 40–55 are being realized in Christ. Dubis acknowledged that the motif also may be seen in the references to Isa 40–55 that are scattered throughout the epistle.

Eric Gréaux claimed that his dissertation was the first comprehensive intertextual examination of the function of the OT in 1 Peter.[79] His thesis was that the OT passages are quoted to evoke the larger context and situation of the original readers and that most of these OT quotations or allusions are taken from sections of the OT with exodus, second-exodus, or diaspora themes as their literary context. Basing his methodology largely on Hays, Gréaux proposed that many of the references to the OT in 1 Peter have a metaleptic function in the epistle, a group of references that include Isaianic texts. The OT texts have the dual function of reminding the readers of their metaphorical status as exiles and exhorting them in the context of suffering. Gréaux concluded that the Isaianic citations and allusions—most of which recapitulate exodus or second-exodus language—function to emphasize the honor and election the audience has in their present context.

Recently, Jocelyn Williams has developed her own methodology for locating and analyzing the intertextual links in 1 Peter.[80] She examined two selected texts in 1 Peter by applying the following methodology, which proceeded with four investigative steps: (1) the presumed source(s) of the texts to be considered, (2) definitions of the *types* of intertextual devices to be considered, (3) questions raised by scholars in the field of biblical intertextuality, and (4) the method to be used in studying the way(s) the Isaianic texts function in the rhetorical structure of 1 Peter. In explanation of the fourth step, she classified the OT references as either quotation or allusion, examined the references for alterations, identified the place of

---

78. Dubis, *Messianic Woes*.
79. Gréaux, "The Function."
80. Williams, "A Case Study," 37–55.

Semiotics and Biblical Interpretation

the references in the rhetoric of Peter's argument, and drew conclusions on Peter's use of these texts for his exegetical and rhetorical methods. Williams's thesis was that a christological reality underlies Peter's rhetoric. Her work is especially helpful for seeing how a clearly stated methodology is applied to the use of the OT in the NT.

Finally, three dissertations have been written recently that require a brief examination here. The major argument of Hyukjung Kwon is that the reception of Psalm 118 in the NT points solely toward Christ and his role in bringing about the new exodus.[81] He concluded that this was the case also for 1 Peter, especially when the singular citation of Psalm 118 in the epistle is viewed together with the allusions to Isaiah 53. Kwon's presentation of a new exodus theme for 1 Peter was not new, but it did provide more support for viewing this concept as the thematic background for the citations and allusions to the OT in 1 Peter. S. A. Woan examined the use of the OT in 1 Peter but highlighted the epistle's use of Psalm 34.[82] While Woan aimed toward terminological clarity in intertextual research, his methodological approach largely follows those of previous studies. Finally, Kenny Ke-Chung Lai examined five Spirit passages in 1 Peter with the aim of proving that Petrine pneumatology can be understood fully in light of Isaiah's new exodus theme.[83] In this work, he erroneously spoke of intertextuality as both a theory and a method. Lai applied only three criteria (following Hays) for recognizing and interpreting citations. Interestingly, Lai did not examine any of the Isaianic citations in 1 Peter.

The importance of this book lies in both the application of a semiotic method for interpreting intertextual references and the treatment of Isaiah in 1 Peter. As the previous discussion has demonstrated, none of the approaches of the works on 1 Peter that examined a second-exodus motif in conjunction with intertextuality did so through a semiotic lens. Moreover, those works that treat the Isaianic references in 1 Peter do so only as one part of their investigation. In this book I will provide a comprehensive examination of the Isaianic references in 1 Peter and will do so through a newly proposed semiotic methodology. My hope is that the application of a semiotic method with intertextual theory will draw the scholarly community closer to a consensus in the way in which intertextual research is done within the realm of biblical studies.

81. Kwon, "The Reception."
82. Woan, "Psalm 34."
83. Lai, "The Holy Spirit."

2

A New Approach to Intertextuality

ANY INTERTEXTUAL INVESTIGATION IS inherently built upon a specific understanding of a text. One's definition of a text, in turn, influences one's definition of textuality. Semiotics approaches a text as a verbal sign complex in which the text is composed of smaller signs and even can be viewed as a system of signs.[1] Textuality, then, would be defined as the production, utilization, and comprehension of texts for signifying purposes. Three criteria of textuality can be identified: context, intent, and structure. All texts are messages within a specific context, are created for communicative purposes, and exhibit coherence in their structure. With these items set forth, the purpose of this second chapter is to lay the foundation for the exegetical work in the following two chapters by constructing a theory of textuality that is based on semiotics. Only with this theory in place can an investigation of the intertextual signs in 1 Peter commence.

A semiotic approach to textuality is founded upon two essential components: the *universe of discourse* and the *encyclopedia*. While Charles Sanders Peirce's triadic sign model has supplied the three main items necessary for semiosis to occur (sign, object, and interpretant), he provided no statement concerning the communicative conditions of sign usage. The universe of discourse provides such conditions. In short, the universe of discourse is the world of the text. The second necessary element for constructing a semiotic theory of textuality is the encyclopedia. An encyclopedia goes beyond the borders of the universe of discourse by including a given society's conventional knowledge. In contrast to the universe of

---

1. This definition is similar to that of Alkier (see "Intertextuality," 7).

discourse, then, the encyclopedia is the immediate world outside the text in which the text is situated.

The survey of pertinent research areas in chapter 1 has outlined how NT scholars have attempted to resolve the methodological problem for investigating the use of the OT in the NT. The methodology for this study will follow the model outlined by Stefan Alkier.[2] His semiotic approach to biblical intertextuality is a recent proposal that claims to provide a common theoretical basis for intertextual studies specifically and NT studies generally. In this chapter, I will begin by narrating the steps of the methodology. Then, in order to situate Alkier's method in its proper context, I will provide a sketch of the thought and works of Charles Sanders Peirce, the individual upon whom the majority of the method is based. The last two sections will examine in further depth the two main terms used in the method: *universe of discourse* and *encyclopedia*. The sections on universe of discourse and encyclopedia are treated separately since both concepts are developed further by Peirce's successors. Finally, the chapter will conclude with a concise description of a semiotic theory of textuality.

A Semiotic Methodology

Alkier applies Peirce's work on semiotics initially by designating texts as linguistic signs. Peirce's three categories are implemented by Alkier in order to examine the diversity of relationships among texts and potential meanings derived therein. The fundamental assumption here is that meaning is generated from interactions among the linguistic signs. Accordingly, Alkier views the derivation of a theory of textuality as the initial step in such a method. Alkier then proposes three perspectives through which one can engage in textual study: intratextuality, intertextuality, and extratextuality. Intratextuality is concerned solely with the internal features of a text such as its literary structure and rhetorical composition. Intertextuality is concerned with the effects of meaning that emerge from the textual relationships. Finally, extratextuality is concerned with the meanings that emerge from references to external signs (e.g., cultural anthropology, archaeology). While Alkier does mention that each perspective can be investigated on its own, his conviction is that intertextual study cannot be done until an intratextual analysis is performed and that extratextual study is dependent—in some form or

---

2. As delineated in Alkier, "Intertextuality," 3–21; and "New Testament Studies," 223–48.

fashion—on the first two perspectives.³ The following is a delineation of the three major steps that will govern the investigation of the data.

Step One: Establish a Theory of Textuality Based on Semiotics

The first step of a semiotic approach to intertextuality that Alkier proposed is the derivation of a theory of textuality that is based on semiotics. This step is crucial since intertextuality is intrinsically part of textuality, and vice versa. Here, semiotics assists in providing the framework for constructing a textual theory. Two fundamental aspects of semiotic theory are examined, the *universe of discourse* and the *encyclopedia*. The term *universe of discourse* was introduced by Peirce in the context of his writings on logic, and it concerns the logical world in which signs can operate. Alkier incorporated the definition given by James Jakób Liska at this point: "The universe of discourse is what an utterer and interpreter must share so that communication can result."⁴ A determination of this concept provides the boundary or border within which signs and objects exist and interact. Regarding texts, Alkier defined the universe of discourse as follows: "The universe of discourse of a given sign connection, for example, of a text, is then the world that this text establishes and assumes so that what is told by or claimed by the text can plausibly function."⁵ In short, the universe of discourse is the world of the text.

An *encyclopedia* "encompasses the conventionalized knowledge of a given society and, thus, breaches the boundaries of individual sign relations by virtue of the concept of the universe of discourse."⁶ Alkier borrowed this term not from Peirce, but from the modern-day semiotician Umberto Eco. Textual signs do not function apart from connections to other external sign systems. For example, the general encyclopedia for the Epistle of 1 Peter is the first-century Jewish and Christian culture. This encyclopedia would differ, however, from the encyclopedia of twenty-first-century America. The importance of this concept is demonstrated in the interpreter's choice of encyclopedia with which to open a text's universe of discourse. In contrast

---

3. Cf. Alkier, "From Text to Intertext," 3; and "New Testament Studies," 240.

4. Alkier, "New Testament Studies," 231. The citation is from Liszka, *A General Introduction*, 92.

5. Alkier, "New Testament Studies," 231.

6. Ibid., 233.

to the universe of discourse, the encyclopedia is the immediate world outside the text in which the text is situated.

In this initial step of the methodology, a history of both the universe of discourse and the encyclopedia will be provided. Both fundamental terms will serve as the basis for establishing the theory of textuality that will govern the study. Also, a semiotic theory of textuality assists in determining the methodological steps for textual and intertextual study.

Step Two: Perform an Intratextual Investigation of 1 Peter

After constructing a theory of textuality based on semiotics, one must determine the realm of investigation. The second step will focus on the intratextual form of investigation. Intratextual investigation is concerned solely with text-immanent relationships. A text-immanent perspective observes the world of the text by inquiring into syntactics, semantics, and pragmatics (i.e., the text's universe of discourse). Syntactics investigates how signs are ordered, and with regard to argumentative texts—of which 1 Peter is an example—the focus of attention would be upon the composition and structure of the argument. Semantics investigates the meaning of signs in the syntactic structure, that is, within the narrow boundaries of the universe of discourse alone. Pragmatics investigates the relation between the text and sign users.[7] Regarding the latter item, the text's universe of discourse and the reader's encyclopedic knowledge interact to produce practical questions concerning the ideology of the text. All questions that move beyond the level of universe of discourse are not addressed here, but in the following step.

Therefore, the three areas of syntactics, semantics, and pragmatics will serve as the three major avenues of investigation for the second step in the methodology. A concluding section will provide summary statements that will detail a precise description of the universe of discourse of 1 Peter. On completing the intratextual analysis, further investigation can begin on the intertextual relationship between 1 Peter and Isaiah.

---

7. See Alkier, "Intertextuality," 8–9; and "New Testament Studies," 241.

Step Three: Perform an Intertextual Investigation of the Use of Isaiah in 1 Peter

Intertextual investigation is concerned with effects of meaning that emerge from the textual relationships. Semiotics allows one to perform three types of intertextual studies: production-oriented, reception-oriented, and experimental. Before describing each type of approach, Alkier distinguished between two ideal types of intertextuality: limited and unlimited.[8] Limited intertextuality examines textual relationships written into the text or those based on signs within the text, and is marked by methodological controls (covering both production- and reception-oriented approaches). Unlimited intertextuality examines texts in relation to the entire universe of texts and is marked by little to no methodological controls (covering both reception-oriented and experimental approaches).

Moving to the three types, the first, production-oriented intertextuality, examines the effects of meaning that result from identifiable texts in the text being interpreted. The task here involves observing which texts are referenced and how this takes place.[9] Second, reception-oriented intertextuality inquires into the historically verifiable interrelation of at least two literary texts. Thus, with this second type one moves from mere identification of an intertext to its function in the text and the meaning it generates. If one approaches this type of intertextuality within an unlimited framework, then this would allow readings for which there is no historical information to be included, such as, "How would an educated Hellenistic Jew in Alexandria in the A.D. 70s have read the letters of Paul?" Finally, experimental intertextuality examines effects of meaning that can arise from reading two or more texts together even if this reading is not grounded in the history of production or reception. For example, a possible experimental approach stemming from the opening citation of Mark's Gospel would be to read Isaiah alongside the Gospel of Mark.

The third and final type of investigation is extratextuality. Extratextual investigation is concerned with the classic introductory issues as well as items relating to textual history, history of literature, social-science approaches, and encyclopedic assumptions from both textual and archaeological signs. Here, texts are used as sources of information. This type of

---

8. Alkier, "New Testament Studies," 242.

9. For this first type, the best-known practitioner would be Richard Hays and his criteria (or seven *tests*) for determining allusive echoes (*Echoes of Scripture*, 29–32).

A New Approach to Intertextuality

investigation prepares the foundation for a plausible construction of encyclopedic knowledge based on text-external signs.

The goal for this third and final step of the methodology is to locate the signs and their objects and then to determine the interpretant for each of these. The interpretant will be governed by the encyclopedia of 1 Peter. Therefore, a description of the encyclopedia of 1 Peter will be provided first, followed by a detailed examination of all the Isaianic signs in 1 Peter.

Three augmentations or limitations will be made to Alkier's proposed method. First, the extratextual perspective will not be examined in this study. The classic introductory issues for 1 Peter are discussed exhaustively in the major commentaries. Thus, the emphasis here will be on the intratextual and intertextual approaches. Second, the experimental type of intertextual study will not be explored in this study due to space limitations; however, some remarks on how this type of intertextual study would apply to the use of Isaiah in 1 Peter will be included in the conclusion of this book. Third, the intertextual perspective will follow only the production-oriented approach for each intertextual sign. The signs will be grouped into two categories: quotations and allusions/echoes.

The Semiotics of Charles Sanders Peirce

C. S. Peirce was involved in numerous areas of research throughout his life. His work took place in the realms of philosophy and logic, semiotics, mathematics, epistemology, metaphysics, and various scientific areas as well. Although Peirce is noted as one of America's greatest philosophical and scientific minds, he considered himself most of all a logician. For this reason, in order to understand his philosophy one must remember that it is embedded firmly in mathematics.[10] Throughout his life Peirce composed around 12,000 pages in published papers and 80,000–100,000 pages of unpublished manuscripts. One of the reasons Peirce's work was neglected for a few decades was due to the fragmentary nature of his writings and their sheer volume. Only during the late 1950s did the sixth and final volume of Peirce's philosophical work come to print.[11] In the 1970s some of Peirce's mathematical works finally were published.

---

10. de Waal, *On Peirce*, 7. Also of note was Peirce's fixation on the number three. Some of the triadic elements in his semiotic theory possibly could be a direct result of this fixation.

11. This effort was spearheaded by two of Peirce's students: Charles Hartshorne and

Defending Hope

When examining Peirce's writings, one must be aware of the major influences upon him and his thought. The following is a brief listing of some of these influences.[12] First, Peirce's upbringing in a Unitarian home took seriously both religion and science as the study of God's works. Second, his exposure to Concord Transcendentalism was an event that predated his reading of philosophy—whether the influence was from Emerson or Kant. Third, and flowing from the previous influence, Peirce was attracted to Kant's work on universal categories through which all objects of knowledge could be analyzed. As will be demonstrated below, Peirce revised Kant's theory into his own "new list of categories." Fourth, Peirce's critique of positivism is very close to what he later would call "pragmatism."[13] A fifth influence is that of the philosophy of John Locke. Peirce single-handedly brought Locke's term (*semiotics*) and his program into wide circulation.

The primary sources for Peirce come from his lectures and unpublished writings; however, his correspondence with Victoria Lady Welby from 1903 to 1911 is especially enlightening. This correspondence is mentioned here because it is known for being one of the best introductions to Peirce's philosophical views and his semiotic theory. Lady Welby was a relatively obscure English philosopher who, from 1885 until her death in 1912, wrote on problems of language and meaning. According to Hardwick, "Her basic thesis was that language follows experience; not the other way around."[14] Lady Welby is purported to have begun the correspondence with Peirce upon reading his entries in a philosophical dictionary. She had her publisher send Peirce a copy of her book *What Is Meaning?* in hopes that she could convert him from semiotics to "significs" (or "sensifics"). *Significs* was her term for her newly developed science of meaning that examined the relationship between sense, meaning, and

---

Paul Weiss. The result was the six-volume series entitled Collected Papers of Charles Sanders Peirce (cited in chapter 1). In 1980, two additional volumes (vols. 7–8) were produced for this collection by Arthur Burks.

12. As outlined by Orange, *Peirce's Conception of God*, 1–24.

13. Many semiotic historians argue that Peirce actually is best known for his "pragmatism" (or "pragmaticism"). In essence, pragmatism holds that the significance of a theory is determined only by its practicality. This aspect of Peirce's work is examined briefly in the discussion of his correspondence with Lady Welby. For further detail on Peirce's pragmatism, see Apel, *From Pragmatism*; Moore, *American Pragmatism*; and Ochs, *Peirce*.

14. Hardwick, *Semiotic and Significs*, xx.

significance.[15] Peirce acknowledged the validity of significs, but he argued that it could be subsumed under his semiotic system as a description of the relation between sign and interpretant.

While neither Peirce nor Lady Welby was effective in converting the other to their own theory, the basic link between the two approaches was their practical implications. According to Danesi, Peirce actually is best known for "pragmatism," a view "which maintains that the significance of any theory or model lies in the practical effects of its application."[16] By contrast, Lady Welby's insistence on significance relates to Peirce's pragmatism. The correspondence between the two philosophers highlights this link while also demonstrating the different subject matter of each viewpoint. The fundamental misunderstanding of both individuals was a result of their approaches: "*Significs* would be better called, as Lady Welby sometimes does call it, *Sensifics*, for its subject matter is sense, while *Semeiotic* is, properly speaking, the theory of the action of signs. Pragmaticism is the link, if any, between the two 'sciences.'"[17] Nonetheless, Peirce's replies to his interlocutor evidenced his distinct views on the classification and typology of signs, which will be examined below.

Having mentioned the various influences upon Peirce's thought and the primary sources for his writings, the discussion now turns to the development and delineation of his semiotic theory. The following aspects are surveyed: the new list of categories, the triadic sign model, Peirce's typology of signs, and the three divisions of a semiotic science.[18] For comparative purposes, references to Peirce's discussion of these topics in his correspondence with Lady Welby are provided as well.

In 1867, Peirce presented a paper to the American Academy of Arts and Sciences entitled "On a New List of Categories." This paper basically was a critique of Kant's universal conceptions (or categories) in which

15. For a fuller discussion of her concept of significs, see Appendix B in Hardwick (167–75), which is a reproduction of her 1911 article "Significs" in *The Encyclopaedia Britannica*, vol. 25.

16. Danesi, *The Quest for Meaning*, 20.

17. Deledalle, *Peirce's Philosophy*, 93. See especially his chapter on the correspondence between Peirce and Lady Welby, 87–99.

18. In general, the discussion progresses through the development of Peirce's semiotic as outlined by Short, *Peirce's Theory of Signs*. In his chapter on the development of Peirce's semiotic, Short stated three purposes for the chapter: to show the flawed nature of Peirce's 1868–1869 doctrine of thought-signs, to demonstrate the influence of theories of mind and knowledge on Peirce's semiotic, and to show that the catalyst that drove Peirce's thinking to develop was his struggle against idealism.

Peirce presented the foundation for his own philosophical thought. Aristotle had derived ten categories, Kant had derived twelve, and now Peirce had condensed and revised this list to three. The following is Peirce's discussion of these three categories, which are referred to as firstness, secondness, and thirdness:[19]

> The ideas of Firstness, Secondness, and Thirdness are simple enough. Giving to being the broadest possible sense, to include ideas as well as things, and ideas that we fancy we have just as much as ideas we do have, I should define Firstness, Secondness, and Thirdness thus: Firstness is the mode of being of that which is such as it is, positively and without reference to anything else. Secondness is the mode of being of that which is such as it is, with respect to a second but regardless of a third. Thirdness is the mode of being of that which is such as it is, in bringing a second and third into relation to each other. I call these three ideas the cenopythagorean categories.[20]

According to Peirce, Firstness merely refers to something that is entirely independent of something else; "it is the category of the unreflected feeling, mere potentiality, freedom, immediacy, of undifferentiated quality and independence."[21] Thus, anything that can be thought of brings with it the idea of something, and this idea is called Firstness. Secondness refers to the idea that something also can be distinguished from another; "it is the category of comparison, facticity, action, reality, and experience in time and space."[22] Thirdness comes from setting two objects in relation to each other; "it is the category of mediation, habit, memory, continuity, synthesis, communication (semiosis), representation, and signs."[23] Peirce's revision of Kant's categories is significant for semiotics because from these categories Peirce developed his theory of signs, particularly his sign model.

---

19. In keeping with Short's argument that Peirce's semiotic thought developed, the citation here is not from Peirce's "New List of Categories" (1867), but from a letter to Lady Welby in 1904. Here Peirce first attributed the names of "firstness, secondness, thirdness" to the conceptions he originally formulated in 1867. Cf. Hardwick, *Semiotic and Significs*, 24–31. Peirce's terminology for these three categories in his 1867 paper was *quality*, *relation*, and *representation*.

20. CP 8:328.

21. Nöth, *Handbook of Semiotics*, 41.

22. Ibid.

23. Ibid.

A New Approach to Intertextuality

Peirce's model of the sign is composed of three distinct elements: a sign or representamen, an object, and an interpretant.

> A sign, or *representamen*, is something which stands to somebody for something in some respect or capacity. It addresses somebody, that is, creates in the mind of that person an equivalent sign, or perhaps a more developed sign. That sign which it creates I call the *interpretant* of the first sign. The sign stands for something, its *object*. It stands for that object, not in all respects, but in reference to a sort of idea.[24]

This triadic sign model can be contrasted with the Sausurrean binary model of signified and signifier. However, Peirce's fundamental understanding of semiotics "is its relational or *functional* character of the sign."[25] The latter comment highlights the importance of the interpretant. As Peirce stated, "Nothing is a sign unless it is interpreted as a sign."[26] Moreover, in his clarification of his understanding of semiosis, Peirce commented that "by 'semiosis' I mean . . . an action, or influence, which is, or involves, a coöperation of *three* subjects, such as a sign, its object, and its interpretant, this tri-relative influence not being in any way resolvable into actions between pairs."[27] This basic proposition on the sign process derives from Peirce's new list of categories: "A *Sign*, or *Representamen*, is a First which stands in such a genuine triadic relation to a Second, called its *Object*, as to be capable of determining a Third, called its *Interpretant*."[28] Thus, one can see the influence of Peirce's epistemological categories upon his semiotic theory.

Peirce referred to the sign as a representamen in that it is the "perceptible object" or "a vehicle conveying into the mind something from without" or "its own material nature."[29] In CP 2:228, Peirce stated that the sign stands for an object at least in one respect, which he sometimes called "the *ground* of the representation." The ground is simply one idea or quality chosen to represent the object. Peirce further elaborated what he meant by an object in distinguishing between two types of objects: immediate and dynamical (or mediate). An immediate object is the object "as the Sign itself represents it, and whose Being is thus dependent upon the Representation

---

24. CP 2:228. Cf. Hardwick, *Semiotic and Significs*, 31–32.
25. Nöth, *Handbook of Semiotics*, 42.
26. CP 2:308.
27. CP 5:484.
28. This citation is from Houser, *Essential Peirce: Volume 2*, 272.
29. CP 2:230; 1:339; 8:333.

of it in the Sign."³⁰ A dynamical (or mediate) object is "the Reality which by some means contrives to determine the Sign to its Representation" or that which "the Sign *cannot* express, which it can only *indicate* and leave the interpreter to find out by *collateral experience*."³¹

The third and final part of the sign triad is the interpretant. The citation from Peirce in 2:228 identifies the interpretant as the sign that arises in the mind from the interaction of sign and object. Some difficulty arises, however, when this definition is compared with another definition Peirce offered only a few years earlier. In this other instance he defined the interpretant as the "idea" produced in the mind: "the idea to which it [the sign] gives rise, [is] its *interpretant*."³² Thus, the interpretant is defined on the one hand as simply an idea created by sign-object interaction and, on the other hand, as a separate sign. If Peirce's semiotic program developed over time, then one would be inclined to take the definition from 2:228 as his final understanding of the interpretant. In this case, the interpretant would be a sign that is created in the mind of the interpreter. Such an understanding would allow for unlimited semiosis.³³ In Eco's discussion of Peirce's concept of the interpretant, he resolved the issue by equating the idea with the actual sign and thus proposed no apparent contradiction in Peirce's understanding of the interpretant. Indeed, Peirce affirmed elsewhere in his semiotic writings the possibility of unlimited semiosis.³⁴

As with the object, Peirce divided the interpretant into its possible manifestations. He distinguished between an immediate interpretant, a dynamic interpretant, and a final interpretant. The immediate interpretant is "the Quality of the Impression that a sign is fit to produce, not any actual reaction."³⁵ In other words, it is the vague connection that determines a sign and object so that the process of semiosis has its inception. The dy-

---

30. CP 4:536. In his correspondence with Lady Welby, Peirce also referred to the immediate object as the "Object within the Sign" (Hardwick, *Semiotic and Significs*, 83).

31. CP 4:536; 8:314. In his correspondence with Lady Welby, Peirce also referred to the mediate object as the "Object outside of the Sign" (Hardwick, *Semiotic and Significs*, 83).

32. CP 1:339.

33. Umberto Eco referred to unlimited semiosis as "infinite regression" (*The Role*, 189). See also his discussion of unlimited semiosis in *A Theory of Semiotics*, 71–72.

34. For example, Peirce stated that a sign is "anything which determines something else (its interpretant) to refer to an object to which itself refers (its object) in the same way, this interpretant becoming in turn a sign, and so on ad infinitum" (CP 2:300).

35. CP 8:315. Cf. Hardwick, *Semiotic and Significs*, 110.

A New Approach to Intertextuality

namic interpretant "is whatever interpretation any mind actually makes of a sign."[36] Whereas the immediate interpretant has an indirect effect upon the interpreter, the dynamic interpretant produces a direct effect. Finally, the final interpretant "is that which *would finally* be decided to be the true interpretation if consideration of the matter were carried so far that an ultimate opinion were reached."[37] Pinpointing the final interpretant would require sufficient consideration and reflection; thus, this type of interpretant is not always apparent in every act of semiosis, unlike the immediate and dynamic interpretants.[38]

The relationship between sign, object, and interpretant has been presented in various diagrammatical forms. A complex, but helpful, figure is one constructed by Eco. In addition to the basic semiotic elements, his diagram includes the ground and the two types of objects as well (see figure 1 below).[39]

Figure 1. Eco's Representation of the Sign Triad

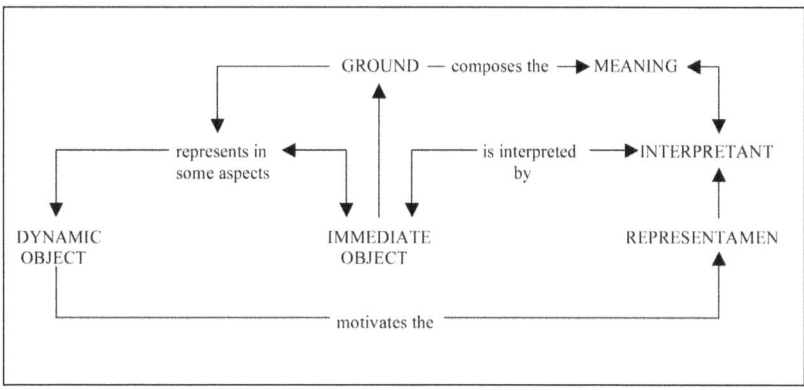

In addition to the inclusion of all of Peirce's elements in the sign triad, Eco's diagram is also helpful in that it demonstrates the place of meaning in Peirce's theory of signs. Initially, a dynamic object supplies the motivation for the production of a sign (representamen). Then, the ground composes meaning by representing (in only some aspects) a dynamic object—which

---

36. Ibid.

37. CP 8:184. Cf. Hardwick, *Semiotic and Significs*, 110.

38. In his correspondence with Lady Welby, Peirce summarized succinctly each of the interpretants: "The Immediate Interpretant is an abstraction, consisting in a Possibility. The Dynamical Interpretant is a single actual event. The Final Interpretant is that toward which the actual tends" (Hardwick, *Semiotic and Significs*, 111).

39. Eco, *The Role*, 183 (used courtesy of Indiana University Press).

takes its form in the sign triad as an immediate object—but this meaning is produced only as a result of the relation between sign and object in the form of an interpretant. According to Eco, "ground, meaning, and interpretant are in fact the same, since it is impossible to define the ground if not as meaning, and it is impossible to define any meaning if not as a series of interpretants."[40] In this sense, meaning can be described as the translation of a sign into another sign-system, since the definition of an interpretant is the sign or idea created in the interpreter's mind.

Another aspect of Peirce's semiotic theory is his development of a comprehensive typology of signs. He began by developing the triadic sign relation of sign, object, and interpretant into three trichotomies, each relating to Peirce's three categories. In sum, Peirce developed four sets of typologies, but much of this discussion in his writings is undeveloped and tentative. Therefore, many modern semioticians attempt to summarize Peirce's writings on sign typologies. The following table is one such summary:[41]

Table 1. Peirce's Sign Trichotomies

Trichotomy / Category	I. of the *representamen*	II. of relation to *object*	III. of relation to *interpretant*
Firstness	qualisign	icon	rheme
Secondness	sinsign	index	dicent
Thirdness	legisign	symbol	argument

From this table one can calculate a possibility of 27 (3^3) classes of signs. However, some classes logically could not be possible; for example, a qualisign can be only iconic and rhematic. The natural restrictions reduce the possible combinations to ten principal classes of signs. Thus, Peirce's writings on the typologies are limited to these ten possibilities.[42]

---

40. Ibid., 184. This notion is confirmed by Peirce, cf. CP 5:179; 5:175; 2:293.

41. Nöth, *Handbook of Semiotics*, 45 (used courtesy of Indiana University Press). Cf. Hardwick, *Semiotic and Significs*, 32–35.

42. The ten principal classes are as follows: qualisign, iconic sinsign, rhematic indexical sinsign, dicent sinsign, iconic legisign, rhematic indexical legisign, dicent indexical legisign, rhematic symbol, dicent symbol, and argument (CP 2:254–63; 8:341). For a concise presentation of these classes and a brief description of each, see Nöth, *Handbook of Semiotics*, 45.

A New Approach to Intertextuality

Of particular interest here is the relation between signs and objects. These three relations—termed *icon, index,* and *symbol*—Peirce referred to as "the most fundamental division of signs."[43] In the following quotation, Peirce briefly defined each of the three divisions.

> Firstly, there are *likenesses*, or icons; which serve to convey ideas of the things they represent simply by imitating them. Secondly, there are *indications*, or indices; which show something about things, on account of their being physically connected with them.... Thirdly, there are *symbols*, or general signs, which have become associated with their meanings by usage. Such are most words, and phrases, and speeches, and books, and libraries.[44]

In other words, icons are signs that result from resemblance (photographs, portraits), indices are signs that result from relation (a pointing index finger, the words *here* and *there*), and symbols are signs that result from convention (a cross stands for Christianity, the color white stands for purity). Peirce devoted much of his writing to an elaboration on these three sign types, and many modern semioticians have utilized these three divisions in their application of a semiotic model.

Finally, in his writings Peirce categorized semiotics as a science that falls under the umbrella of the philosophic sciences (phenomenology, normative sciences, and metaphysics).[45] In Peirce's estimation, semiotics has three branches of study: semiotic grammar, critical logic, and universal rhetoric. Semiotic grammar is concerned with the formal conditions of signs, that is, their basic components, types, and classification. The goal of this branch is "to ascertain what must be true of signs in order for them to embody meaning."[46] The second branch, critical logic, is concerned with the necessary conditions for signs to represent their object truthfully. According to Peirce, critical logic examines those conditions "without the fulfillment of which [signs] would not be signs of the object intended (that

---

43. CP 2:275. Peirce's earliest typological list was provided in 1867 in his paper "New List of Categories." This typology consisted only of icon, index, and symbol.

44. CP 2:281, 285.

45. For a helpful diagram of Peirce's system of sciences, see Liszka, *A General Introduction*, 4. Peirce divides the theoretical sciences into formal, physical, and psychical. Semiotics is a suborder of philosophy, which in turn is a class under the formal sciences. For an explanation of the role of semiotics in the larger system of sciences, see Liszka, 7–9.

46. Liszka, *A General Introduction*, 10. Cf. CP 1:191; 2:206, 229.

is, would not be true)."⁴⁷ Finally, universal rhetoric is concerned with the general conditions for signs to act as vehicles of communication. The aim of this branch includes studying the conditions under which signs are developed, communicated, and interpreted.

Much more could be stated about Peirce's work in the realm of semiotics, but to do so would go beyond the scope of this work. Nevertheless, the elements of his philosophical and semiotic thought have been presented here as a basic introduction to his thought. With this introduction in place, the foundation is set for a description of the two major components of a semiotic theory of textuality: the universe of discourse and the encyclopedia.

Universe of Discourse

The term *universe of discourse* was introduced by Peirce in the context of his writings on logic and concerns the logical world in which signs can operate. A careful reading of his work, however, reveals that this term did not originate with Peirce. He indicated his indebtedness to two nineteenth-century logicians, Augustus De Morgan and George Boole. De Morgan first utilized the term in 1846. He described the "universe" strictly as the name that can be applied to a proposition (or the "universe of a proposition").⁴⁸ Four years later De Morgan expanded his description of the universe as "the whole universe of thought, or a conceivably separate portion of it."⁴⁹ Boole holds pride of place for being the first to introduce the construction under examination in this section (universe of discourse); though, compared with De Morgan, Peirce mentioned Boole only in passing.⁵⁰ Most of the occurrences of *universe* in Peirce's work are in the context of mathematics and logic.

Peirce noted a distinction in De Morgan's understanding of the universe of discourse: it can be limited or unlimited. A limited universe of discourse is only what actually occurs, whereas an unlimited universe of discourse includes the realm of the logically possible. In reference to the latter, Peirce stated that "our discourse seldom relates to this [unlimited] universe: we are either thinking of the physically possible, or of the historically existent, or of the world of some romance, or of some other limited

---

47. This citation is from Robin, *Annotated Catalogue*, MS 1147A: 111.
48. Houser, *Writings*, 474. Cf. De Morgan, "On the Syllogism, I," 379–403.
49. De Morgan, "On the Syllogism, II," 79–127.
50. See Boole, *An Investigation*. For Peirce's positive appraisal of Boole, see Fisch, *Writings*, 223–24, 404–5.

universe."[51] So, when Peirce wrote of the universe he was referring mostly to the nuance of limitation. Some common phrases he used for this universe were "the universe of possibility," "the universe of possible objects," and "the possible species in the universe."

So how exactly did Peirce define the universe of discourse? In the course of expounding on the nature of semiosis as communication, he defined the universe of discourse as follows: "In every proposition the circumstances of its enunciation show that it refers to some collection of individuals or of possibilities, which cannot be adequately described, but can only be indicated as something familiar to both speaker and auditor."[52] His understanding of the universe of discourse is related closely to another term he utilized called the *commens*. The commens is the common sense world that is shared by the one who creates the sign and the one who interprets the sign. The shared knowledge by both utterer and interpreter is necessary "in order that the sign in question should fulfill its function."[53] Peirce also suggested that the universe of discourse is gained through collateral experience, or "the previous acquaintance with that the sign denotes."[54] In summary, the universe of discourse is the common ground between utterer and interpreter that provides the boundary or border within which signs and objects exist and interact. As such, it is an essential concept when studying any act of semiosis.

James Jakób Liszka, in his introduction to the semiotic theory of Peirce, stated that the universe of discourse more appropriately can be termed the "discourse community."[55] With the use of this term, Liszka indicated that the world shared by both the utterer and interpreter is a sort of common community that allows for genuine communication to take place. His idea of a discourse community is indeed a development of Peirce's notion of collateral experience. The interpreter must have a previous acquaintance with the idea or conceptual world to which the sign refers. One of

---

51. Kloesel, *Writings*, 451. Peirce described the unlimited universe similarly when discussing the algebra of logic (ibid., 170).

52. CP 2:536.

53. Hardwick, *Semiotic and Significs*, 197. Cf. CP 4:117; and also Fisch, *Writings*, 153. Peirce further escribed the commens by relating it to "that mind into which the minds of the utterer and interpreter have to be fused in order that any communication should take place" (Hardwick, 196–97).

54. CP 8:179.

55. Liszka, *A General Introduction*, 92. This concept is similar to Prewitt's position on semiosis and communication (see the discussion of his work in chapter 1).

Peirce's examples, which Liszka includes as well, is the role of the universe of discourse of the proposition "Hamlet was mad": "One must know that men are sometimes in that strange state; one must have seen madmen or read about them; and it will be all the better if one specifically knows . . . what Shakespeare's notion of insanity was."[56] A correct interpretation of the proposition or sign requires at the very least a grasp of the psychological state of madness. However, a nuanced understanding of Shakespeare's notion of madness (if even he has one) would be ideal.

Nathan Houser argued that Peirce's idea of the interpretant in the sign triad demonstrates the necessity of an interpretive community. Houser's line of argumentation is as follows: since advanced thought makes use of symbols and since symbols are based on convention, "all advanced thinking depends on one's participation in a linguistic or semiotic *community*."[57] Houser attributed this general conclusion to Peirce due to the latter's stress on community as a theme throughout his writings. Moreover, Houser proposed that Peirce, as his thought developed, became more and more adamant about the integral role of community (or collateral experience) in the interpretation of signs. Houser asserted that Peirce "regarded the *identification with community* as fundamental for the advancement of knowledge (the end of the highest semiosis) and, also, for the advancement of human relations."[58] The emphasis on a community of interpretation points to the fundamental aspect of the universe of discourse as the shared or common ground between utterer and interpreter.

Alkier provided the most articulate explanation of how Peirce's universe of discourse applies to an analysis of textual signs. Regarding texts, Alkier defined the universe of discourse as follows: "The universe of discourse of a given sign connection, for example, of a text, is then the world that this text establishes and assumes so that what is told by or claimed by the text can plausibly function."[59] This definition coheres with Peirce's description of the concept. A text's universe of discourse includes all the signs introduced by the text as well as assumptions about the world and reality. For example, the physical world portrayed in J. R. R. Tolkien's *The Lord of the Rings* refers to a different world than that portrayed in any is-

---

56. CP 8:179.

57. Houser and Kloesel, *The Essential Peirce*, xl.

58. Ibid. The concept of community is the basis for Alkier's approach to miracle texts in Paul's writings as well (*Wunder und Wirklichkeit*, 55).

59. Alkier, "New Testament Studies," 231. Cf. ibid., "Intertextuality," 8.

A New Approach to Intertextuality

sue of *National Geographic*. The latter even would lose its credibility if it portrayed orcs and trolls as part of the physical world. Thus, a sign occurs within a specific universe of discourse, and a determination of this universe is necessary for semiotic interpretation.

By its very nature the universe of discourse places limits on signs and their function. Since the universe represents a clearly defined realm, limitations are placed not only on the scope of statements—in this case, linguistic signs—but on the validity of statements as well.[60] Each act of writing is a separate world unto itself. A semiotic investigation first must reconstruct the respective universe of discourse in order to know its boundaries. Alkier claimed that the scope of a universe of discourse can be determined differently depending on the object of investigation. For example, he suggested that one could examine the universe of discourse of a collection of writings (e.g., the Pauline corpus), a single writing (e.g., Galatians), or a section of a text (e.g., the opening of Romans).[61] Therefore, the universe of discourse can be set narrowly or widely. In addition, it always refers to a concrete text, which contrasts with the abstract notion of the encyclopedia that will be examined in the next section.[62] A construction of the universe of discourse is essential in that it provides the framework in which signs operate and the context in which they are to be interpreted.

In *Wunder und Wirklichkeit*, Alkier illustrated how the universe of discourse is constructed. He investigated the function of miracles in six of the Pauline Letters.[63] He introduced the study with a few chapters on methodology in which he makes his semiotic method explicit. Then he supplied an exegetical examination for each of the six epistles. Each of these chapters is devoted essentially to an elaboration of the universe of discourse of each epistle. Thus, the content centers on the occurrences of miracles in each text and the conception of reality that is presupposed. The common thread of each exegetical chapter is the initial section entitled "Die Eröffnung des Diskursuniversums: Der Lektürevertrag."[64] Here Alkier examined briefly the epistolary introductions in order to construct the universe of discourse

---

60. Alkier, New Testament Studies," 232.

61. In *Wunder und Wirklichkeit*, Alkier took the third option and examined each of Paul's epistolary introductions to construct the universe of discourse for each epistle.

62. Alkier, *Wunder und Wirklichkeit*, 78.

63. Ibid., 9. The six epistles are 1 Thessalonians, Galatians, 1 Corinthians, 2 Corinthians, Philippians, and Romans.

64. A possible translation is, "The Opening of the Universe of Discourse: The Reading Contract."

Defending Hope

and, thus, to determine the world which the text assumes. As the subtitle of this section indicates, Alkier held that the prescript contains an implicit *reading contract* between the author and reader. The prescript functions to open the universe of discourse to the reader.[65]

In the chapter on 1 Thessalonians, Alkier suggested that the universe of discourse allows for the reality of miracles. In 1 Thess 1:1 the human world (ἐκκλησίᾳ) and the divine world (θεῷ, Ἰησοῦ Χριστῷ) are linked together, and this connection indicates at the outset of the epistle that something extraordinary can be expected. He states that "Absender und Adressaten sind verbunden mit dem Gott, der Tote erwecken kann und Jesus Christus tatsächlich von den Toten erweckt hat" and "nur unter dieser Prämisse ergibt ihre Kommunikation Sinn."[66] Moreover, the current rule of Jesus (1 Thess 1:10) requires an acceptance of God's ability to perform miracles. So the reading contract of 1 Thessalonians, which is located in the epistolary introduction, is based on an acceptance of the reality, not the possibility, of miracles. The information derived from the epistolary introduction provides the framework in which the signs can operate. After constructing the universe of discourse, Alkier then located the textual signs concerning miracles in the epistle and discussed how each should be interpreted within the borders of the universe of discourse.

In conclusion, the universe of discourse is defined as the realm of the physically possible or historically existent that encompasses the shared knowledge of both utterer and interpreter. Precisely this shared knowledge is crucial for signs to fulfill their communicative function. The universe of discourse provides the boundaries or borders within which signs and objects exist and interact. When one examines texts as signs, the universe of discourse is the world established by the text that provides the structure and context in which signs operate.

---

65. Alkier connects the prescript and universe of discourse in the introduction to the exegetical section of his book. He proposes that "das Präskript eröffnet das jeweilige Diskursuniversum, indem es einen Lektürevertrag zwischen dem impliziten Autor und dem impliziten Leser initiiert" (*Wunder und Wirklichkeit*, 90). A possible translation of this quote is, "The prescript opens the respective universe of discourse by initiating the reading contract between the implicit author and the implicit reader."

66. Alkier, *Wunder und Wirklichkeit*, 92. A possible translation is, "Sender and receiver are united with God, who is able to awaken the dead, and Jesus Christ, who actually awoke from death" and "only from this premise does their communication yield significance."

Encyclopedia

The *encyclopedia* is a term Alkier borrowed not from Peirce but from modern-day linguists and semioticians. The term has had mixed reception among literary theorists, especially as it relates to the term *dictionary*. Both terms represent competing models that are set forth to explain how texts are produced and understood. In order to arrive at a definition of an *encyclopedia*, the discussion below will begin by comparing and contrasting *dictionary* and *encyclopedia*. Much of the debate over these two terms took place in the early 1980s, so emphasis will be on the groundwork laid during this time period. The section will conclude with Alkier's application of the theoretical nuances of *encyclopedia* to linguistic texts/signs and some pertinent examples of how this concept can be utilized in textual studies.

Three individuals were prominent in the *dictionary* vs. *encyclopedia* debate: John Haiman, William Frawley, and Umberto Eco. At the time Haiman's article was published in 1980, most linguists held to a distinction between a dictionary and an encyclopedia.[67] The former generally is associated with semantics, while the latter is associated with pragmatics. In other words, dictionaries are concerned with cognitive meaning (that is, they are independent of experience), whereas encyclopedias are concerned with emotive or referential meaning (or meaning that is conditioned by culture and experience).[68] Haiman related this commonly accepted position as follows: "Knowledge of (the semantics of) a language—properly codified in a dictionary—is distinct from that knowledge of the real world which belongs in an encyclopedia alone."[69] After acknowledging this commonly held position, Haiman then indicated that it was his primary object of criticism.

If one were to look up the entry for *horse* in a dictionary, one would find only selected information about a horse, such as a basic description and possibly a sketch of a horse. The point Haiman made here is that one will not find every possible piece of information about a horse in a dictionary; a more detailed entry could be found in an encyclopedia, which would include items such as metaphors, images, and idioms associated with the word. At a cursory glance, then, the dictionary is brief for practical purposes only. Haiman explored whether or not a theoretical basis exists for deciding

---

67. See Haiman, "Dictionaries and Encyclopedias," 329–57.

68. Therefore, the method of a dictionary is to relate words to other words. On the other hand, an encyclopedia relates words to extralinguistic facts.

69. Haiman, "Dictionaries and Encyclopedias," 330.

what information to include in a dictionary. He asked, "Where exactly does one stop?" and "Why does one stop?" His view is that a distinction between a dictionary and an encyclopedia is impossible and misconceived. In short, Haiman argued that dictionaries *are* encyclopedias.

Haiman aimed to blur the distinction between various elements associated with both terms. His argument is structured by an examination of six contrasts that commonly are set forth to distinguish dictionary and encyclopedia. The contrasts are as follows: linguistic and cultural knowledge, subjective and objective fact, essence and accidence, semantics and pragmatics, analysis and synthesis, and proper names and common names. The first member of each pair corresponds to dictionaries, whereas the second member of the pair corresponds to encyclopedias. Haiman's ultimate conclusion is that the common distinctions among these six pairs are arbitrary and without significance because every word or concept is tied to some sort of reality. As he stated, "Semantic knowledge derives from cultural knowledge."[70] Therefore, a distinction between dictionary and encyclopedia is ill founded. Haiman's work is significant because of his challenge to this fundamental—and often assumed—distinction.

On the other hand, Frawley, Haiman's primary interlocutor, adamantly reasoned that Haiman failed to blur the distinctions between the two terms.[71] Frawley's rebuttal emphasizes the weaknesses of Haiman's arguments, that is, the latter's penchant for oversight, oversimplification, and paradox. The basis for Frawley's dismissal of the supposed blurring of distinctions lays with his suggestion that Haiman is an adherent to "a new bandwagon position against rationalism and universal grammar."[72] In effect, Haiman subsumed the dictionary under the encyclopedia.

Haiman offered a brief rejoinder to Frawley in which he sought to clarify his own position.[73] Here he returned to the questions he posed in his first article. Haiman wondered why the inclusion of information in a dictionary entry was limited in comparison to an encyclopedia. If the reason is primarily practical and not theoretical, then dictionaries are in fact encyclopedias and no distinctions should be made between the two. His main point was that meaning should not be restricted to information found in a dictionary because "to define 'meaning' so narrowly as to exclude this

70. Ibid., 355.
71. See Frawley, "In Defense," 53–61.
72. Ibid., 55.
73. Haiman, "Dictionaries and Encyclopedias Again," 353–55.

A New Approach to Intertextuality

'extra-linguistic or social information' may satisfy some lofty prerequisites but it utterly fails to describe English or any other natural language."[74] Umberto Eco shares the viewpoint of Haiman.

In the discussion above, the comment was made that linguists associate a dictionary with semantics and an encyclopedia with pragmatics. In other words, a dictionary pertains to the ideal and the theoretical whereas an encyclopedia pertains to actual experience. In Eco's view, however, a theory of semantics should be concerned not with the ideal but with the actual. He drew upon the theory of N. L. Wilson and suggested "a semantic theory ought to concern not the ideal competence of an ideal speaker, but the factual beliefs that people share about things. Meanings are common social beliefs, sometimes mutually contradictory and historically rooted, rather than undated and theoretically fixed constructs."[75] So the information found in a dictionary entry is actually a special type of encyclopedic entry in which is contained "the actual cultural definition that a society conventionally accepts for a given content unit," which also is referred to as the "common core of factual beliefs."[76] The theory espoused by Wilson—and supported by Eco—draws no essential differences between dictionary and encyclopedia.

Wilson's theory has led Eco to the understanding that the dictionary is an illusion. A dictionary is not merely subsumed under an encyclopedia. On the contrary, "The dictionary is dissolved into a potentially unordered and unrestricted galaxy of pieces of world knowledge. The dictionary thus becomes an encyclopedia, because it was in fact *a disguised encyclopedia*."[77] Even though Eco discarded the theoretical idea of a dictionary, he did state that representations found in a dictionary can be useful. He suggested that the common distinction between dictionary and encyclopedia should be reversed. Thus, the dictionary is pragmatic and the encyclopedia is semantic.

So, what is the import of an encyclopedia for a semiotic understanding of textuality? If a text (or a linguistic sign) is composed and received in a context or culture, then the encyclopedia is the framework of cultural knowledge and conventions that provide understanding for such a context. Alkier defined an encyclopedia as something that "encompasses the conventionalized knowledge of a given society and, thus, breaches the boundaries of individual sign relations by virtue of the concept of the universe

---

74. Ibid., 354.
75. Eco, *A Theory of Semiotics*, 99. Cf. Wilson, "Linguistic Butter."
76. Eco, *A Theory of Semiotics*, 99.
77. Ibid., *Semiotics and Philosophy*, 68.

of discourse."[78] Textual signs do not function apart from connections to other external sign systems. For example, the general encyclopedia for the Epistle of 1 Peter is the first-century Jewish and Christian culture. In this context the epistle was composed and disseminated. A first-century Jewish or Christian encyclopedia would differ, however, from the encyclopedia of twenty-first-century America.

An important issue in the interpretation of textual signs is the question of which encyclopedia to open when examining a text. Should a reader choose one's own current encyclopedia or the one in which the text was created? Various answers are provided for this question. While any reader certainly is free to read a text with any encyclopedia in mind, doing so would create an unlimited semiotic interpretation of a particular textual sign. Indeed, the majority of semioticians allows for and even practices such an approach to textual signs. Eco, however, argued against unlimited semiosis and for a distinctly limited approach:

> Once Borges suggested that it would be exciting to read the *Imitation of Christ* as if it were written by Celine. The game is amusing and could be intellectually fruitful. I tried: I discovered sentences that could have been written by Celine ("Grace loves low things and is not disgusted by thorny ones, and likes filthy clothes..."). But this kind of reading offers a suitable "grid" for very few sentences of the *Imitatio*. All the rest, most of the book, resists this reading. If, on the contrary I read the book according to the Christian medieval encyclopedia, it appears textually coherent in each of its parts.[79]

Borges, a twentieth-century Argentine writer, basically suggested that Thomas à Kempis's fifteenth-century work be read through the lens of a different encyclopedia than the one in which it was composed (Celine was a twentieth-century French writer). In this example, Eco provided justification for the view that examining a text through the encyclopedia in force at its composition provides a coherent, if not correct, interpretation of that text. If one follows the Augustinian notion that linguistic signs are a direct result of human intention—where intentionality points to sign production for the purpose of communication—then one must choose the encyclopedia which corresponds to the context of the sign's genesis.

---

78. Alkier, "New Testament Studies," 233. Cf. also idem, *Wunder und Wirklichkeit*, 72–73, 78.

79. Eco, *The Limits of Interpretation*, 59–60.

A New Approach to Intertextuality

In Alkier's work on miracles in Paul's letters, he articulated the role of texts in a culture's encyclopedia in the following statement: "Ein gegebener Text ist . . . ein Ausschnitt aus dieser virtuellen Enzyklopädie."[80] Texts are fragments of the culture (Kulturfragment) in which they are produced, and the encyclopedia functions as the reference point (Bezugspunkt) for their interpretation.[81] After his exegetical work on the universe of discourse of Paul's letters, Alkier discussed what could be determined about the encyclopedia of Pauline Christianity in relation to miracles. Paul's writings reveal that although miracles were not a normal part of everyday life, certain situations arose in which they occurred (those of danger, disease, and the establishment of new churches). Alkier concluded: "der Wunderdiskurs im paulinischen Christentum erhält seine Kohärenz durch die intertextuelle Anknüpfung an die Enzyklopädie des Judentums, und zwar insbesondere der Schöpfungstheologie."[82] His work demonstrated that the encyclopedia of Judaism is incorporated into Paul's letters through the use of intertextual references. Therefore, to understand Paul's writings on miracles, one must first comprehend the intertextual references to the Exodus event and the birth of Isaac, to name just two examples.

Alkier also cautioned against generalizing the results of one text's encyclopedia to that of another text. For example, his work on miracles in Paul's writings exists only as a smaller portion of the larger encyclopedic entry that could be entitled *Miracles in Early Christianity*.[83] Semiotic studies of the Gospels and other early Epistles would contribute further to this larger encyclopedic entry. Thus, the entry is not exhausted but merely treated in as much depth as Paul's letters will allow.

Another example of the use of encyclopedia in biblical interpretation is Leroy Huizenga's examination of the Gospel of Matthew through its Jewish encyclopedia.[84] His emphasis is on Matthew's allusions and thematic echoes to Isaac (Genesis 22) and how Isaac typology in this Gospel presents Jesus

---

80. Alkier, *Wunder und Wirklichkeit*, 70. A possible translation is, "A given text is . . . an excerpt from this virtual encyclopedia."

81. Ibid., 72.

82. Ibid., 304. A possible translation is, "The miracle discourse in Pauline Christianity receives its coherence by means of the intertextual connection to the encyclopedia of Judaism, and indeed particularly to creation theology."

83. As the title of chapter 10 communicates, "Wunder: Einträge in die Enzyklopädie des paulinischen Christentums" (or "Miracle: Entries in the Encyclopedia of Pauline Christianity").

84. Huizenga, "The Matthean Jesus," 63–81.

as the new Isaac. Huizenga's investigation is based on the understanding that "meanings of texts exist only as interpreted in culture."[85] In this way he followed the encyclopedic model set forth by Haiman and Eco, but he proposed that historical investigation of an OT intertextual reference should focus not on the OT context, but on the context in which the reference was generated. Huizenga offered a strong warning against scholars who assume that a plain meaning of canonical OT texts was agreed upon in the first century. Thus, the majority of Huizenga's work centers on a thorough survey of the Isaac tradition from the OT period to the first century A.D. He concluded that the significance of the Suffering Servant figure in Isaiah is overestimated and should even be relegated to a secondary interpretation below that of the Isaac figure.

Huizenga has demonstrated the importance of the encyclopedia and how it functions in the semiotic interpretation of texts. One can see how Huizenga's choice of the Jewish encyclopedia led him to the interpretation that the Isaac tradition was the backdrop for Matthew's portrait of Jesus. Such an interpretation contrasts with conclusions that might be reached if one chooses to open Matthew's Gospel with a Christian encyclopedia. Consequently, the interpreter of a text is faced with a decision as to which encyclopedia should be used to open the text. Huizenga stated, "the question for Christians involves which encyclopedias permit adequate and authoritative religious readings of the canonical texts."[86] A related question is whether or not the conclusions reached from opening multiple encyclopedias are mutually exclusive. The choice of encyclopedia is most pertinent for intertextual references. Should the encyclopedia of the NT document hold pride of place over the encyclopedia that governs the OT reference? Should both encyclopedias be examined and compared? Perhaps the universe of discourse could serve as a corrective at this point for varying interpretations.[87]

In conclusion, the encyclopedia is a semiotic concept that encompasses the cultural knowledge and conventions in which a sign is situated. The encyclopedia differs from the universe of discourse in that the former represents the world outside the text. If encyclopedias and dictionaries are not distinguished on a theoretical basis, then the encyclopedia contains both semantic and pragmatic elements. Linguistic signs (or texts) are viewed as

85. Ibid., 65.

86. Ibid., 81.

87. Eco suggested that the logical limit for every encyclopedia is governed by the universe of discourse (*The Role*, 189).

fragments of the larger cultural context, and an investigation of semiotics of texts can assist one in reconstructing the respective encyclopedia. While a text can be opened with any encyclopedia, a proper interpretation of the sign involves determining which encyclopedia was in force during the creation of the sign and using this encyclopedia to examine the text. Selecting the proper encyclopedia proves to be a significant issue for intertextual studies.

Summary: A Semiotic Theory of Textuality

Semiotic theory defines a text as a verbal sign complex. A text is composed of smaller signs and even can be viewed as a system of signs. Within this verbal sign complex are linguistic signs that always stand in relation to an object with the result of producing an interpretant. Here the semiotic program of Charles S. Peirce provides a detailed model for identifying, understanding, and interpreting signs. The correlative understanding of textuality can be described as the production, utilization, and comprehension of texts for signifying purposes.

The universe of discourse and the encyclopedia are essential components of a semiotic textual theory because they constitute the two spheres that allow signs to function. Alkier relates this point by stating that a sign "requires at least two relationships in order to function: It must belong to a currently perceptible sign structure and at the same time to a culture as the whole of its virtual signs connections."[88] The perceptible sign structure is the universe of discourse and the cultural relation is the encyclopedia. Both of these concepts match the criteria for textuality that were mentioned at the outset of this chapter. The encyclopedia meets the criterion of context, the universe of discourse meets the criterion of structure/coherence, and the criterion of intent is met through the basic assumption of semiotic theory that signs are created for the purpose of communication.

How is a semiotic textual theory exhibited in an investigation of intratextual and intertextual perspectives of a text? While the answer to this question is the goal of the next two chapters, it will suffice here to provide some preliminary methodological comments. Intratextuality concerns only the internal relationships within a text; thus, this perspective essentially involves the construction of a text's universe of discourse (or the world *of* the text). Intertextuality concerns relationships between a text and other

---

88. Alkier, "New Testament Studies," 330.

texts; thus, this perspective builds upon an intratextual investigation but is governed by the encyclopedia of the text (or the world *outside* the text). In each approach to a text, the linguistic signs are the vehicles that carry meaning. With the theoretical foundation in place, an investigation of the signs can commence.

3

The Textual Universe of 1 Peter

THE SEMIOTIC INVESTIGATION OF Isaiah in 1 Peter will begin first with a construction of the world of the text, that is, the universe of discourse of 1 Peter. This intratextual investigation involves a construction of the world established by that text. The universe of discourse encapsulates the common ground between the author and the reader that provides the borders within which signs and objects both exist and interact. For this study, the primary objects of investigation are the Isaianic signs that appear in 1 Peter. To understand how the author utilizes the Isaianic signs, one first must be familiar with the world 1 Peter establishes. Therefore, in this chapter the entire epistle will be examined with the goal of determining the structure and context in which the Isaianic signs within can operate.[1]

Alkier's delineation of an intratextual approach is based on a threefold division of semiotic analysis: syntactics, semantics, and pragmatics.[2] The present chapter is structured according to this threefold division. Syntactics investigates how signs are ordered. Regardless of the text's genre (whether narrative, argumentative, or poetic), the syntactic analysis examines the structure and composition of the text. Alkier offered literary-critical structuralism and ancient rhetoric as two possible models of analysis for this

---

1. Cf. Alkier, *Wunder und Wirklichkeit*, 9.

2. The three divisions were introduced and developed extensively by the semiotician Charles Morris. His notable works on semiotics include *Foundations of the Theory of Signs* and *Signs, Language and Behavior*. Morris presented syntactics, semantics, and pragmatics as the three branches of semiotic study. Liszka argued that Morris's nomenclature actually derives from the three divisions proposed by Peirce: semiotic grammar, critical logic, and universal rhetoric (*A General Introduction*, 10).

step. Then the semantic analysis involves a location of the signs and their meaning within the syntactic structure. Reading signs in this way is based on a limited line of questioning that excludes encyclopedic knowledge. Finally, pragmatics investigates the relationships between signs and their users. The pragmatic analysis is "the attempt to perceive the ideology of the text and to formulate the reasons for my rejection or agreement."[3] In the course of this type of analysis, one's encyclopedic knowledge begins to confront the universe of discourse. As a result, questions arise that cannot be dealt with on the level of universe of discourse and must be examined either intertextually or extratextually.

In an intratextual investigation, all forms of encyclopedic knowledge are placed in the background and the text is examined as an autonomous unit. As Alkier stated, "Here, one investigates the text in question under the widest possible methodological shielding from encyclopedic knowledge."[4] In other words, the world presented by the text should be accepted uncritically. The concern here is not so much the accuracy of the information the text presents, but precisely *what* is presented and *how* it is presented. The following investigation will follow the order of steps outlined by Alkier and will conclude with a summary description of the universe of discourse of 1 Peter.

Syntactics

In a syntactical analysis the aim is to determine how the signs are ordered or structured. The emphasis in this step falls not on the signs themselves, but on the larger document and how it is constructed. The two primary approaches to the structure of 1 Peter are based on ancient epistolary conventions and ancient rhetorical conventions.[5] Each approach has its own method for determining the structure of the epistle; thus, some variation exists in the respective structural divisions. Although the method of rendering the structure is different for these two approaches, both hold in

---

3. Alkier, "New Testament Studies," 241.

4. Ibid., "Intertextuality," 9.

5. Proponents of a structural outline based on epistolary conventions include Michaels, *1 Peter*; Davids, *First Epistle of Peter*; Marshall, *1 Peter*; Achtemeier, *1 Peter*; Martin, *Metaphor and Composition*; Elliott, *1 Peter*; Jobes, *1 Peter*; Feldmeier, *First Letter of Peter*; and Donelson, *I and II Peter and Jude*. Proponents of a structural outline based on rhetorical conventions include Thurén, *Rhetorical Strategy*; Campbell, *Rhetoric of 1 Peter*; and Witherington, *Letters and Homilies*.

common an assumption of the literary unity of the final form of the text. In general, proposals concerning the structure of 1 Peter are dependent on two items: the unity and the genre of the letter.

The majority of current scholarship views 1 Peter as a unified text. Under this view the various composite theories of source critics from the early twentieth century are rejected. Such theories emphasized the awkward placement of a doxology at 4:11, a different understanding of persecution following 4:11, and the presence of numerous references to baptism. All three of these issues would point to 1 Peter as a compilation of various literary works. B. H. Streeter observed the distinctions on persecution and proposed that 1 Peter was composed of two letters: the first (1:1—4:11) speaks of persecution as potential, while the second (4:12—5:14) speaks of persecution as actual.[6] The doxology of 4:11 corroborates this position as it formally signals the end of the first letter. F. L. Cross suggested a variation on this theory. He argued that the frequent occurrences of suffering (πάσχω) and the term's close connection with the word for Passover (πάσχα), combined with a juxtaposition of *joy* and *suffering* in the epistle, identified 1 Peter as part of a paschal liturgy.[7] For Cross, then, the context for suffering is not persecution, but the Easter season.

Another item used to support the composite nature of 1 Peter is the multiple allusions to baptism in the first half of the epistle.[8] Herbert Preisker—following R. Perdelwitz's theory from 1911—articulated that 1 Peter is a baptismal homily converted into an epistolary format.[9] Moreover, he identified the actual point in the letter where the baptismal candidate would receive baptism as occurring between 1:21 and 1:22. Marie-Émile Boismard contributed to the baptismal homily theory by locating four distinct hymns in the epistle that would have been used during the homily for the baptismal candidate.[10]

---

6. Streeter, *The Primitive Church*, 128-31.

7. Cross, *Paschal Liturgy*, 31.

8. Achtemeier, *1 Peter*, 58, summarized the baptismal allusions as follows: "In addition to the use of the word itself (3:21) and references to new birth (1:3, 23), allusions to early baptismal ritual were found in references to milk (2:2, in early ritual combined with honey), light (2:9), the baptismal formula (1:23-25), the role of the celebrant (2:25), and the putting off of ornamentation (3:3)."

9. Preisker, *Die katholischen Briefe*, 156. Cf. also Perdelwitz, *Die Mysterienreligion*, 37.

10. Boismard, *Quatre hymnes*.

Defending Hope

More recent scholarship has examined the evidence of the composite theories and has found it to be unpersuasive. A major argument against these theories is the lack of manuscript evidence supporting any of them. Perhaps the most extensive treatment of factors supporting the unity of 1 Peter is offered by John Elliott.[11] He examined nine major indicators of structure (the epistolary framework, announcement of themes, inclusions, chiasms, transitions, commencement indicators, conclusion indicators, compositional patterns, and link-words), a few of which are discussed here for illustrative purposes. The epistolary framework (1:1–2 and 5:12–14) brackets the epistle with similar terms, images, and themes that occur frequently throughout 1 Peter. Themes are announced in three sections of the epistle that receive further treatment in subsequent sections (1:1–2d; 1:3–12; and 2:11–12). Inclusions, or the use of similar terms or images at the beginning and ending of a unit, can be found embracing larger units (e.g., "suffering for a little while" in 1:6 and 5:10 brackets the body proper of 1:3—5:11), smaller units (e.g., "elect" in 2:4–10), and within subunits or verses (e.g., "honor" in 2:17). The transition from indicative statement to imperative command occurs often throughout each chapter of 1 Peter, thus reflecting an intentional pattern. Finally, Elliott listed at length the various link-words (terms, motifs, or themes that join units or verses together) in the epistle, and these are significant in that they extend the line of thought introduced by the author.[12] In view of an intratextual approach to the structure of 1 Peter, the literary unity of the document will be assumed.

The genre of 1 Peter is generally accepted as an epistle exhibiting the typical epistolary conventions of the first century and similar to the epistolary structure that characterizes the Pauline corpus. However, one varying viewpoint on genre, which functions as a subgenre of epistle, is set forth by J. Ramsey Michaels.[13] Based on apocalyptic elements in the epistle and the similarities it exhibits with other diaspora letters (e.g., James [1:1]; the Jerusalem Council letter [Acts 15:23–29]), Michaels suggested that 1 Peter is "an apocalyptic diaspora letter to 'Israel.'"[14] The apocalyptic elements

---

11. See Elliott, *1 Peter*, 68–80.

12. Interestingly, Elliott's discussion of compositional patterns (*1 Peter*, 74–77) resembles the work of rhetorical critics on 1 Peter.

13. See Michaels, *1 Peter*, xlvi–xlix. Another sub-genre of epistle that fits the composition of 1 Peter is that of an encyclical or circular letter, which is supported by the epistle's opening address to multiple locations. For this view see Schutter, *Hermeneutic and Composition*, 17.

14. Michaels, *1 Peter*, xlvi.

The Textual Universe of 1 Peter

certainly are present and are affirmed by many scholars, but the supposition that the apocalyptic diaspora letter was a distinct genre has been challenged.[15] Of interest here is not necessarily whether Michaels's theory is plausible, but how his view of the genre of 1 Peter might affect a structural analysis. Interestingly, the structural outline Michaels offered is no different than the resulting outlines of epistolary analyses.

Alkier proposed that a semiotic method frequently allows for the incorporation of existing methodological approaches.[16] A syntactic approach to the structure of a text is one area to which this conviction applies. In the three subsections below, the structure of 1 Peter will be outlined according to both epistolary and rhetorical approaches, and comparisons will be made.[17] A justification for the syntactical structure of 1 Peter will be offered, as well as the outline adopted for this study. Additionally, insights from semiotics will be provided on how the structure of the text factors into one's location of and interpretation of the signs within.

The Epistolary Structure of 1 Peter

First Peter is notoriously difficult to structure based on content alone. The author weaves ideas together gradually as opposed to marking distinctly his change of topic. Moreover, topics already discussed are broached at a later point, indicating that no theme is ultimately closed. Paraenetic sections are frequently intertwined with theological statements. Thus, a rendering of the letter's structure based on content is difficult at best. Most Petrine scholars emphasize two primary features in presenting a structural outline of 1 Peter: linguistic structures and epistolary conventions.

Michaels pointed out that the structure of 1 Peter is marked out in the broadest sense by the two plural vocatives, ἀγαπητοί ("dear friends"), located in 2:11 and 4:12.[18] From this linguistic marker there appear to be at least three main sections of the epistle: 1:1—2:10; 2:11—4:11; and 4:12—5:14. The predominance of imperative mood verbs in 1:13—2:10,

---

15. See especially Davids, *First Epistle of Peter*, 13–14.

16. Alkier, "New Testament Studies," 224.

17. The purpose of this syntactic approach is simply to set forth the framework in which the signs exist. While comparisons will be drawn between both structural representations, the subsections are not meant to be exhaustive, as these structural approaches are addressed at length in other works.

18. Michaels, *1 Peter*, xxxiv.

a verb form not used before 1:13, prompted Achtemeier to conclude that 1:13—2:10 is the first main section of the epistle body.[19] In addition, he argued that the use of διό in 1:13 indicates that what comes before this section should be labeled the introduction to the letter or the *prooemium*. The presence of these linguistic markers assists one in determining a general structural framework for 1 Peter.

Conventions of the epistolary genre comprise the second major element for constructing an outline of 1 Peter. When NT letters are examined against their first-century Greco-Roman background, similarities in form and structure can be discerned.[20] The structural categories that both Greco-Roman letters and NT letters hold in common—but are not necessarily found in every letter—are an opening address, a blessing, a well-wishing formula, a thanksgiving, a main body, and a conclusion. A uniqueness of Christian letter writers in the first century is their modification and adaptation of the opening and closing formulas to suit the needs of their addressees.[21] Outside of an opening and closing formula, NT letters exhibit a large degree of variance in the main body section. For this reason, the only definitive findings that can be drawn from comparative studies are limited to broad structural divisions.

Epistolary conventions complement the linguistic structure, as proposed above by Michaels, by setting off an opening, a closing, and a blessing from the main body of the epistle. The revised structural outline would take shape then as follows (see table 2 below): opening or prescript (1:1–2), blessing or introduction (1:3–12), body opening (1:13—2:10), body middle (2:11—4:11), body closing (4:12—5:11), and closing or postscript (5:12–14). Achtemeier notes here that this structure reflects that which is found in Paul's letters, the latter as the primary object of comparison with first-century Greco-Roman epistles.[22]

The majority of Petrine scholars outline 1 Peter based on the common structural categories found in first-century ancient letters; however, some differences are present among the proposed structural outlines. In

---

19. Achtemeier, *1 Peter*, 73.

20. Pertinent studies on the theory and practice of ancient letter writing include White, *The Form*; idem, *Ancient Letter Writing*; Stowers, *Letter*; White, *Ancient Letters*; Malherbe, *Ancient Epistolary Theorists*; and Richards, *Letter Writing*. For a specific application of the findings of the aforementioned works to NT epistles, see Klauck, *Ancient Letters*.

21. Stowers, *Letter*, 21.

22. Achtemeier, *1 Peter*, 73.

The Textual Universe of 1 Peter

table 2 below, some of the epistolary outlines of 1 Peter are presented for the purpose of comparison. The general structure consisting of prescript, three main body sections, and postscript is used as the basis for comparison. Sections that diverge from this broad division are noted with an asterisk and are discussed below.

Table 2. A Comparison of Epistolary Outlines of 1 Peter

Proponent / Broad Outline	Michaels Davids Jobes Feldmeier[A]	Achtemeier	Martin[B]	Marshall	Donelson	Elliott
Prescript	1:1–2	1:1–2	1:1–2	1:1–2	1:1–2	1:1–2
First Section	1:3–2:10	*1:3–12	*1:3–12	*1:3–12	*1:3–12	1:3–2:10
		1:13–2:10	*1:13–5:12	1:13–2:10	1:13–2:10	
Second Section	2:11–4:11	2:11–4:11		*2:11–3:12	*2:11–4:6	*2:11–12
				*3:13–5:11	*4:7–5:11	*2:13–3:12
						*3:13–4:6
						*4:7–11
Third Section	4:12–5:11	4:12–5:11				4:12–5:11
Postscript	5:12–14	5:12–14	*5:13–14a	5:12–14	5:12–14	5:12–14
			*5:14b			

A. Feldmeier's structure corresponds but with the exception that he labeled 2:11–5:11 as one unit (22). His subdivisions agree with the division of this large unit at 4:11.

B. In Martin's approach to the structure of 1 Peter he took an epistolary outline as the starting point but then moves toward a compositional or rhetorical approach for the larger body section. Thus, he is a unique example but is included here for comparative purposes.

The structural outlines presented above are only the main divisions and do not include subsections. Michaels, Davids, Jobes, and Feldmeier are individuals who follow the broad epistolary outline for 1 Peter. As far as the commonalities among all six outlines, all of them designate

Defending Hope

a prescript and a postscript.[23] Moreover, if one went one sublevel into the main outlines presented above, all the proponents set off a blessing section at 1:3–12. Thus, the majority of variation occurs in the main body sections of the epistolary structure.

Achtemeier, Martin, Marshall, and Donelson all separate the blessing or introduction section (1:3–12) from the main body of the epistle. Martin preferred to follow a general outline of the body and entitles it the "Letter-body," which has a body-opening (1:13), a body-middle (1:14–5:11), and a body-closing (5:12).[24] Marshall proposes three main sections, but differs in the break between sections two and three (at 3:12 as opposed to 4:12). Likewise, Donelson breaks sections two and three differently, but does so at 4:6. Finally, Elliott's structure, while divided in numerous places, differs only in regard to the second main section. Instead of keeping 2:11—4:11 as one unit, he identifies 2:11–12 as a transitional device and then delineates three smaller sections.

A cursory glance at the epistolary outlines of 1 Peter reveals that the majority of Petrine scholars affirm the general outline presented in the second column, with minor variations. The structural divisions take into account a prescript (which includes the naming of the author and recipients and a brief greeting), a postscript (with a closing admonition and greetings), an introductory section or blessing, and three main body sections. When the epistolary conventions are examined in conjunction with the two plural vocatives (ἀγαπητοί), which function as key linguistic markers, the general structure of 1 Peter becomes more evident. Viewing the epistle in this way provides a logical structure in which to examine the signs therein.

The Rhetorical Structure of 1 Peter

A few major writers in the past twenty years have proposed that an epistolary analysis of 1 Peter exhibits major flaws regarding issues of form and structure. Barth Cambell stated that an epistolary analysis "can identify basic parts of the letter (prescript; body-opening, middle, and closing; and

---

23. The only difference on this point is that Martin begins the prescript at 5:13 instead of 5:12 (74–79). He identifies 5:12 as the body-closing. Following this is the greeting section (5:13–14a) and then the farewell (5:14b).

24. Martin, *Metaphor and Composition*, 69–75. Martin's literary analysis of the metaphors in 1 Peter lead him to divide up the structure of the body-middle into three sections corresponding to Marshall's divisions: 1:14—2:10; 2:11—3:12; and 3:13—5:12 (Ibid., 266).

The Textual Universe of 1 Peter

postscript), and their termini, but it cannot account for the composition of the letter-body."[25] While 1 Peter is commonly designated as a paraenetic letter, rhetorical critics attack this claim on the basis that the paraenetic genre does not exhibit a fixed form. Martin supports this argument and concludes that "the identification of 1 Peter as a paraenesis does not provide an explanation of its compositional structure."[26] Ben Witherington III, another proponent of a rhetorical approach, ties these issues back to a fundamental conviction of rhetorical studies: their orality.[27] Since letters were meant to be read aloud to their intended recipients, an epistolary outline can help only in analyzing how letters begin and end. All three of these individuals sought to rectify the difficulties of epistolary analysis by utilizing a rhetorical approach to the structure of 1 Peter.

Martin's rhetorical approach to the structure of 1 Peter focuses on a chief or controlling metaphor and three metaphor clusters. His argument is that the ontological metaphors that describe the status of the readers and the ensuing exhortations supply the basis for a compositional analysis of the letter.[28] The chief or controlling metaphor of the Diaspora (cf. 1:1) combines with the three metaphor clusters to form the basic division of the body-middle. The metaphor clusters are (1) the οἶκος-cluster, the elect household of God (1:14—2:10); (2) the παρεπίδημος/πάροικος-cluster, aliens in this world (2:11—3:12); and (3) the παθήματα-cluster, sufferers of the dispersion (3:13—5:11). According to Martin, the rhetorical situation is set up by the Diaspora metaphor and points to the author's purpose in writing (to encourage a suffering and scattered people). Moreover, the metaphor clusters provide a precise delineation of the epistle's rhetorical structure.

Campbell offers the first comprehensive rhetorical investigation of 1 Peter. His analysis of 1 Peter is based on classical rhetorical criticism, an approach stemming from Greco-Roman rhetorical standards in the handbooks of the Greek and Latin rhetoricians.[29] Under this approach items

---

25. Campbell, *Rhetoric of 1 Peter*, 20. Here he summarizes Martin, *Metaphor and Composition*, 75.

26. Martin, *Metaphor and Composition*, 270.

27. Witherington, *Letters and Homilies*, 46.

28. Martin, *Metaphor and Composition*, 270–73.

29. Definitive introductions to classical rhetorical criticism are Kennedy, *New Testament Interpretation*; and Mack, *Rhetoric*. Drawing on the works of the Greek and Latin rhetoricians, Kennedy (13–14) identified the five major parts of rhetoric as invention (the planning of a discourse and the arguments used within), arrangement (the composition of the parts into a whole), style (choice of words, formation of sentences, and use of

such as the rhetorical unit (the object of study), the rhetorical situation (the situation which both prompts and controls the rhetorical response), and the rhetorical problem (the issue at hand) are examined. Also, classical rhetorical criticism applied to the NT carries over distinct terms for the division of a literary work. In addition to rhetorical features, Campbell also examined sociological concepts of honor and shame as the context of the rhetorical situation of 1 Peter.

The result of Campbell's work is the first full-fledged rhetorical outline of 1 Peter. He identifies an epistolary prescript (1:1–2), an exordium (1:3–12), three arguments (1:13—2:10; 2:11—3:12; 3:13—4:11), and a peroration (4:12—5:14). The structural analysis does not appear much different from the epistolary outlines given above; however, the sub-divisions of each main section reveal the influence of rhetorical criticism. First, the exordium is the introduction of matters that will be discussed, but the exordium also includes establishing the speaker's ethos and gaining the goodwill of the audience. Second, each major argument is subdivided into *propositio* (setting forth what is to be proven), *ratio* (the reason and basis for the proposition), *confirmatio* (the proof of the reason corroborated with additional arguments), *exornatio* (embellishment used to enrich and adorn the argument), and *conplexio* (conclusion and drawing together of the parts of the argument). Finally, the peroration (argument summary) includes the *expolitio* (an examination of an idea from various angles) on suffering, a farewell speech of exhortation (5:1–11), and the closing greeting (5:12–14).

Nearly ten years following Campbell's work, Witherington's socio-rhetorical commentary on 1 Peter is an attempt to refine the previous rhetorical efforts in the epistle, and, like Campbell, includes insights from social-scientific criticism.[30] The structural outline proposed by Witherington differs from Campbell's outline and is as follows: epistolary prescript (1:1–2); exordium (1:3–12); *propositio* (1:13–16); five arguments (1:17—2:10; 2:11—3:12; 3:13—4:11; 4:12–19; 5:1–5); *peroratio* (5:6–9); closing doxology (5:10–11); and epistolary postscript (5:12–14). Witherington contends that Campbell's inclusion of a proposition to introduce each argument does not follow the typical structural pattern. Instead, "the proposition for the whole discourse would come at the end of the exordium and before all the

figures), memory (preparation for delivery), and delivery (control of the voice and use of gestures).

30. One difference between the two is that Witherington moved beyond honor/shame concepts and thus is more comprehensive in his sociological application.

arguments on behalf of the proposition."[31] A second point of disagreement with Campbell lies with the parameters of the peroration. Witherington argued that 4:12—5:14 is too long a section to function as the peroration. Therefore, once the postscript is taken out, he suggests 5:6–9 is the peroration and views the section from 4:12 to 5:5 as two arguments. Themes of hope for the future and self-control that are present in the proposition are echoed in the peroration.

For ease of viewing the exact differences among the three outlines mentioned above, table 3 below illustrates the rhetorical outlines in tabular format. Since Martin's structure is the least developed, his outline will serve as the point of comparison for Campbell and Witherington. Additionally, the outlines are in chronological order from left to right so that one can view the development and refinement of the subsequent outlines. The sections listed in parentheses are pertinent subdivisions included for comparative purposes.

---

31. Witherington, *Letters and Homilies*, 48.

Defending Hope

Table 3. A Comparison of Rhetorical Outlines of 1 Peter

Proponent	Martin	Campbell	Witherington
Rhetorical Outline	1:1–2 Prescript	1:1–2 Prescript	1:1–2 Prescript
	1:3–12 Blessing	1:3–12 Exordium	1:3–12 Exordium
	1:13 Body opening	1:13–2:10 Argument 1	1:13–16 *Propositio*
	1:14–2:10 The οἶκος cluster		1:17–2:10 Argument 1
	2:11–3:12 The παρεπίδημος/ πάροικος cluster	2:11–3:12 Argument 2	2:11–3:12 Argument 2
	3:13–5:11 The παθήματα cluster	3:13–4:11 Argument 3	3:13–4:11 Argument 3
		4:12–5:14 Peroration	4:12–19 Argument 4
		(4:12–19) (*Expolito* on suffering)	5:1–5 Argument 5
		(5:1–11) (Exhortation)	5:6–9 *Peroratio*
		(5:12–14) (Closing and greeting)	5:10–11 Closing doxology
	5:12 Body closing		5:12–14 Postscript
	5:13–14a Greeting		
	5:14b Farewell		

Like the epistolary outlines of the previous section, all three of the rhetorical outlines exhibit no differences in the opening and closing structure of 1 Peter. All identify a prescript, exordium or introduction, and a postscript. Further, the second argument or section for each outline is the same (2:11—3:12). The major differences come in the material before and after this second main section. Campbell's first and second arguments correspond almost exactly with Martin's first two cluster sections, but Campbell breaks down Martin's third cluster section into two parts: a third argument and a peroration. As was noted above, Witherington disagreed with Campbell's inclusion of a proposition for each argument and places the proposition at the front of all the arguments. Finally, Witherington divides Campbell's peroration into four sections: two arguments, a peroration, and a closing doxology.

A cursory glance at three rhetorical outlines of 1 Peter reveals a fair amount of agreement on the first two major sections of the epistle. On the other hand, major differences remain among the structural analyses of the section from 3:13 to 5:11, especially 4:12—5:11. Nonetheless, rhetorical outlines of the structure of 1 Peter offer another viable framework for situating the textual signs, which utilizes known rhetorical conventions and views the orality of a document as foundational to its composition.

Summary

A syntactical analysis of the signs in 1 Peter opens up various approaches to the structure of the text. Here the value of a semiotic method is demonstrated, as it allows for the incorporation of different methodological approaches. For 1 Peter the two major approaches to structure—epistolary and rhetorical—were examined. When one contrasts the outlines produced by both approaches, the similarities and differences become apparent. In addition to the prescript and postscript, there is almost universal agreement on the introductory section (1:3-12) and the first main section of the body (1:13—2:10). The second and third body sections (2:11—5:11) of the epistolary format are construed differently in the rhetorical outlines. Here most of the epistolary outlines break at 4:11, whereas all three of the rhetorical outlines break at 3:12.[32]

A comparative analysis of these two structural approaches to 1 Peter is helpful because it provides the basic framework for examining the content of the epistle. Based on the syntactical insights from both approaches, the following broad structural outline will be the one adopted for this study: 1:1-2 (prescript); 1:3-12 (introductory section); 1:13—2:10 (first body section); 2:11—3:12 (second body section); 3:13—4:11 (third body section); 4:12—5:11 (fourth body section); and 5:12-14 (postscript).

---

32. The exceptions for an epistolary approach are Marshall and Elliott. Donelson breaks the section at an entirely different place (4:6).

Defending Hope

Semantics

A semantic analysis examines the meaning of the signs within the framework of the syntactic structure. Whereas the previous section focused on the Epistle of 1 Peter as a whole, this section will examine the words (or signs) of the text themselves and how they function in the syntactic order. The proposed structure of 1 Peter presented above will serve as the framework for examining the signs. Each section of the structure will be analyzed for what it assumes about the world and reality. Another goal here is to determine, if possible, where the intertextual references are located and how they function in the syntactic order. After examining the semantic relationships of the signs, one will be closer to constructing the universe of discourse of 1 Peter.

One other matter must be mentioned before beginning the analysis. At the level of the universe of discourse the semantic analysis allows one to inquire about the marked relations to other texts (e.g., quotations/citations) and the function of these marked relations in the text's structure. What cannot be investigated, however, is whether or not the quoted text exists or from where it comes.[33] To do so would be to move beyond the borders of the text's universe of discourse. As Alkier has suggested, the danger of moving beyond the text to matters of encyclopedic knowledge must be avoided in this step. Instead, a limited line of questioning will govern the analysis.

Prescript (1:1–2)

The prescript of an epistle is extremely significant for determining the universe of discourse of a text. As Alkier has demonstrated, a prescript

---

33. On this point, see Alkier, "From Text to Intertext," 4. In this article he examined Matthew 1 through both an intratextual and an intertextual approach. Under a discussion of the universe of discourse of Matthew 1, he pointed out that "the genealogy is not an intertextual phenomenon, however, the fulfilment quotation in Mt 1:22f is one" (4). Alkier argued that at this stage of a semiotic investigation the differences between Matthew's genealogy and Luke's genealogy—or the issue of the incompleteness of Matthew's genealogy—are not of importance. Indeed, this would actually go beyond the borders of the universe of discourse and move into issues brought forth from encyclopedic knowledge. The citation in Matt 1:22–23 can be examined within the borders of the universe of discourse only because it is marked as coming from somewhere else (here, διὰ τοῦ προφήτου). On the other hand, the prophet cannot be identified as Isaiah nor can the citation be identified as coming from Isa 7:14; this identification can be done only when one accesses encyclopedic knowledge.

The Textual Universe of 1 Peter

has the ability to initiate the implied world of the text and even can introduce the *reading contract* between author and reader.[34] Common knowledge about the world that may be assumed on the part of the author can be determined from the opening prescript. In the prescript of 1 Peter, a description of author and recipients is provided along with a statement on the latter's current situation, which is supplemented with a theological explanation. Additionally, thematic emphases that will recur throughout the epistle are introduced.

In 1:1, both the author (Πέτρος) and the recipients (ἐκλεκτοῖς παρεπιδήμοις) are named. The only definitive description of the author that can be made is that his name is Πέτρος and he is an ἀπόστολος Ἰησοῦ Χριστοῦ. As for the recipients, both their identity (elect strangers) and their location (διασπορᾶς, "of the diaspora") are generic; however, the geographical location of the diaspora is made slightly more specific with the indication that they reside in Pontus, Galatia, Cappadocia, Asia, and Bithynia (though an exact identification of these areas is possible only by accessing the encyclopedia). Also, the identification of them as elect highlights their distinct Christian character.

The highly debated term παρεπιδήμοις can be understood only as a literal designation at this point—not figurative or metaphorical.[35] The ones in the diaspora are literal strangers in the named regions in 1:1. Thus, at the outset of the epistle the recipients are described in terms of a paradoxical expression: on the one hand, they enjoy an elevated status with God as *elect*; but on the other hand, they are in a vulnerable societal position experiencing the low status of *strangers*. In other words, Peter highlights the vertical dimension (elect) and the horizontal dimension (strangers) of their identity as Christians. Understanding the paradoxical nature of the recipients' situation is crucial, as it will be addressed throughout the epistle.

Verse 2 supplies essential information about the recipients' situation through the use of three prepositional phrases. First, the situation of the recipients is described as "according to the foreknowledge of God the Father." The fatherhood of God points to the rebirth of believers (1:3, 23; 2:2); they have been born into a new family in which God is the father and they are the children (1:14). God also exhibits foreknowledge (πρόγνωσιν). Not only has the paradoxical situation of the recipients not

---

34. See Alkier, *Wunder und Wirklichkeit*, 91–93.

35. See Jobes, *1 Peter*, 61–62 for a concise discussion of the major viewpoints on this word.

escaped God's attention, but as a father figure God has the ability to demonstrate his protection over them (1:5; 5:6–7, 10) or to use their situation as a means for discipline or refinement (1:7). Furthermore, this metaphorical designation of God as Father alludes to subsequent references to the Christian community as the "household of God" (2:4–10; 4:17). Second, the sanctification that occurs through the Spirit provides another description of their status as elect strangers. The recipients are elect by means of the Spirit and the sanctifying work that he effects, and this sanctifying work may point to the qualities of holiness and purity that follow (1:19, 22). Finally, the phrase εἰς ὑπακοὴν καὶ ῥαντισμὸν αἵματος Ἰησοῦ Χριστοῦ indicates the cause (with εἰς taken as causal) of their election by God. Thus, it is precisely the obedience of Christ and the sprinkling of his blood that are the cause of Christian election.

The prescript ends with a greeting of χάρις and εἰρήνη. In relation to the aforementioned situation, *grace* could refer to the gift of God's election and *peace* the result of this election. Since the author states his desire for these qualities to be multiplied in them, perhaps the greeting functions as either a prayer of supplication or a call for them to draw upon the grace offered by God and the peace that comes from being in his family.

From the first two verses of the epistle several important concepts can be discovered about the universe of discourse of 1 Peter. Both author and recipients are connected through Jesus Christ. Peter, the author, is an apostle of/from Jesus, and the recipients are elect because of the obedience of Jesus. In this assumed world, the audience is undergoing a paradoxical predicament as elect or chosen by God, but also as strangers in the world. The Spirit is the source of the sanctification of the audience, that is, the source of their status as holy and set apart. Finally, the world of 1 Peter is one in which God has foreknowledge and is the father of the Christian family or household. In these two short verses, Peter opens up the universe of discourse of his letter with a distinctly theological perspective. The centrality of God, Jesus, and the Spirit is applied to the recipients' status both as elect before God and as strangers in the world.

Introduction (1:3–12)

In the introductory section of the epistle, the identity of each of the named parties in the prescript (with the exception of Peter) is expanded. In addition to being called father again (1:3), God is described as merciful (1:3), life giver (1:3), and powerful (1:5). If God is the implied person behind the testing mentioned in 1:6-7, then it would follow that he is the one who sends trials for the purpose of testing and refining. Jesus is revealed as Lord, and his resurrection is the basis for the living hope into which believers are born (1:3). Not only has Christ been resurrected, but he also will be revealed (1:7), and at this revealing he will make known the result of the recipients' faith. The Spirit is mentioned in the concluding verses as τὸ ... πνεῦμα Χριστοῦ (1:11) and as πνεύματι ἁγίῳ (1:12) who was sent from heaven and is the source of direction behind the preaching of the gospel.

Of particular interest concerning the recipients is the emphasis on their salvation (1:5, 6, 9, 10). In 1:5 this salvation is mentioned as something which will be revealed in the last time (ἐν καιρῷ ἐσχάτῳ), that is, something not yet consummated. Nonetheless, the fact of their salvation, in addition to all that is stated in vv. 3-5, is a cause for rejoicing despite their present circumstances (1:6). Again, in 1:9 salvation is offered as the basis for rejoicing since it is in fact τὸ τέλος τῆς πίστεως. The discussion then shifts in vv. 10-12 to the role of the OT prophets in the salvation that comes through Christ. Accented here is the unique place that the believers hold over against the prophets (who were in fact serving them, 1:12a) and the angels (who long to look into such things, 1:12c). The frequent occurrence of this topic in such a short passage emphasizes its importance. Therefore, one can anticipate that the salvation of the recipients will be a concept always at the foreground of Peter's discussion.

The introduction section of 1 Peter adds to the universe of discourse fundamental beliefs about God, Jesus, and the Holy Spirit and their activity in the world. Furthermore, the situation of the recipients is portrayed—once again in a paradoxical manner—as both an instance of testing and a cause for rejoicing. The author draws on both their experience of salvation and their unique status as believers as a positive antidote to their trying circumstances.

First Body Section (1:13—2:10)

In the first section of the body, Peter begins incorporating citations to substantiate comments on the recipients' identity and their suggested Christian behavior. The first subsection (1:13—2:3) is almost entirely a discourse on how they should live in the world, whereas the second subsection (2:4-10) is an elaboration of their identity as God's chosen people. Moreover, this

Defending Hope

distinction is suggested by the presence of six imperative mood verbs in the first section (1:13, 15 [2], 17, 22; 2:2) and none in the second section.

Peter offers a succinct but powerful transition into the main body in 1:13. The command to hope (ἐλπίσατε) is rooted in foundational elements presented in the introductory section (1:3, 7). Similarly, the call to be holy (ἅγιοι . . . γενήθητε and ἅγιοι ἔσεσθε) is rooted in their identity as "obedient children," which corresponds to being part of God's family (1:1) and modeling Christ's obedience (1:2). Here the command to imitate God's holiness is supported with the citation of an outside source introduced with the phrase διότι γέγραπται ("for it is written," 1:15). While at the intratextual level one cannot determine the referent for this citation, Peter uses it to substantiate his command by basing it in God's divine command.

Other key semantic connections are found in 1:17–21. The recipients are encouraged to conduct themselves (ἀναστράφητε) in fear/reverence during their time of living as resident aliens (παροικίας). The latter term, while somewhat different in meaning than παρεπίδημος, points to their estranged situation (1:1).[36] In the prescript, the blood of Christ was introduced as a key factor in their election (1:2); here in this section the blood of Christ is also the basis for their redemption (1:18–19) and, thus, serves as the reason for conducting their lives in reverence.

The exhortation to love one another constantly (ἀγαπήσατε, 1:22) is grounded in God's merciful act of giving them new birth (1:23; cf. 1:3). Here Peter further defines this new birth as having its source in imperishable seed (ἐκ σπορᾶς . . . ἀφθάρτου) through the living and enduring word of God (διὰ λόγου ζῶντος θεοῦ καὶ μένοντος). Interestingly, the identification of new birth in this section as coming from the word of God contrasts with Peter's previous definition of new birth in 1:3, which states that new birth comes from the resurrection of Jesus Christ. The imperishable seed of God's word also contrasts with the perishable seed associated with human procreation (1:23). At this point, Peter once more supports this proposition with a citation introduced by διότι ("for," a shortened form of the introduction in 1:16). The citation runs from 1:24 to 1:25 and no indication is given

---

36. A detailed treatment of both πάροικος and παρεπίδημος is provided by Elliott, 1 Peter, 457–62. Both terms are subsets of the broad terms for strangers. They describe "persons displaced from their own homes and places of birth and belonging, and live as 'by-dwellers' (par-oikoi, par-epidemoi) among the homes (oikoi) and countries (demoi) of others, with whom they share no kinship or cultural ties" (458). Elliott further distinguished the terms by noting that παρεπίδημος refers to a transient stranger while πάροικος denotes the permanent residence of a stranger.

as to where it is located. While this reference connects with Peter's discussion of imperishable/perishable seed and the word of God, a connection also is made to the close of the introductory section (1:12).

Finally, the first subsection closes with a metaphorical directive. As babies desire physical milk, so they should desire (ἐπιποθήσατε, 2:2) pure spiritual milk. In doing so, they will grow into salvation. Such a portrayal of their salvation matches the understanding of salvation presented in 1:5: they have experienced salvation (implied in 2:2), but have not yet fully attained it (1:5; 2:2). The metaphor continues in 2:3 where Peter indicates they already have "tasted" (ἐγεύσασθε) that the Lord is good. Mention of the Lord in 2:3 provides the point of transition into the second subsection.

The identity of Peter's audience is the sole focus of the section from 2:4–10. In 2:4–8 they are described in detail as a spiritual household, and this description is supported with quotations. First, the Lord (the antecedent of ὅν is ὁ κύριος [2:3]) is designated as chosen by God and as a living stone. The author has previously attributed an elect status to his audience, but now he claims that Jesus also is chosen. He then makes the connection between the audience and Jesus by describing them as living stones (2:5). All this is for the purpose of being a holy priesthood (2:5; cf. 2:9). Peter appeals to Scripture to remind them of their faith in Jesus as the living stone. Verse 6 begins with the introductory formula διότι περιέχει ἐν γραφῇ ("for it stands in Scripture"), and the citation runs through the end of the verse. In modern editions of the Greek text, the font is altered in some way to signify the presence of intertextual references in 2:7 and 2:8, although at the intratextual level this connection cannot be made.[37] Regardless, vv. 7–8 are further commentary on Jesus as the cornerstone. The subsection ends climactically in 2:9–10 with at least seven different phrases describing the audience's identity as the elect people of God.[38] These descriptions combine with the household imagery of 2:4–10 to offer a comprehensive portrait of God's chosen people, which echoes that of 1:1–7.

A couple of trends can be observed regarding Peter's references to other texts in this first section of the body. First, he follows a pattern of discourse (or command) followed by citation. This pattern was the case in all three of the discernible citations (1:13–15, 22–25; 2:4–6). Second, the formulas used

---

37. For instance, the UBS4 edition of the Greek text signifies a reference to the OT by placing the text in bold face type.

38. The seven phrases are as follows: chosen people, royal priesthood, holy nation, God's possession, called out of darkness and into light, the people of God, and those who have received mercy.

to introduce the citations are never the same. The three formulas used are διότι γέγραπται, διότι, and διότι περιέχει ἐν γραφῇ. Even though the formulas vary, the consistent pattern of discourse then citation is helpful in determining where a citation might occur elsewhere in the epistle.

In summary, a few more features of the universe of discourse of 1 Peter can be delineated. First, in this universe God the Father demands holy behavior of his children that is in accordance with his own identity. Second, citations to other texts are crucial to the message communicated by the author due to both their frequency and their function as supporting evidence for statements made in the discourse. Third, the familial metaphor is illustrated further as the recipients are identified with Christ as elect members of a spiritual household.

Second Body Section (2:11—3:12)

First Peter 2:11 signals a clear break in sections with the endearing use of the vocative ἀγαπητοί. Following this vocative noun are five passages addressed to different groups among the audience on how to conduct themselves as members of God's household. Each subsection, except for the fifth, is marked off by a vocative noun. The resulting outline is as follows: to the beloved or to all (ἀγαπητοί, 2:11–17); to the slaves (οἰκέται, 2:18–25); to the wives (γυναῖκες, 3:1–6); to the husbands (ἄνδρες, 3:7); and to all (τὸ δὲ τέλος πάντες, 3:8–12).

In view of the unique situation in which the audience find themselves, specific advice is needed as to how they should interact with the world around them. Peter refers to their status as strangers in the world in 2:11 by including two descriptive terms used previously in the epistle: πάροικος (1:17) and παρεπίδημος (1:1). Already this group has been commanded to live holy lives (1:15–16) in reverent fear (1:17). In 2:11 the exhortation to abstain from evil desires is added to these commands. The second main body section essentially is an exposition of these commands. Peter provides a specific blueprint of how they should live in their context, not only to the group as a whole, but to those who are slaves, wives, and husbands as well.

In 1 Pet 2:11–17, five imperative mood verbs set the tone for the ethical admonitions in the other subsections. The recipients are commanded to submit to every human authority (ὑποτάγητε, 2:13), to honor all men (τιμήσατε, 2:17), to fear God (φοβεῖσθε, 2:17), to love the brotherhood (ἀγαπᾶτε, 2:17), and to honor the king (τιμᾶτε, 2:17). Submission is urged

The Textual Universe of 1 Peter

in the first three cases. All are to submit to every human authority: slaves are to submit to their masters (whether good or evil), and wives are to submit to their husbands (believer or unbeliever). Husbands are called to "live with" (συνοικοῦντες) their wives in a way that would exhibit love and honor (3:7). Finally, all are urged to "be of one mind" (ὁμόφρονες), thus exhibiting love for the brotherhood.

Of note in this second body section are two instances where intertextual references are possibly present. First, in the address to the slaves, Peter offers Christ as an example of suffering (2:21) and shifts to a description of this suffering (2:22-24). Editions of the Greek text signal a citation in 2:22; however, from the literary context and at the intratextual level a determination as to whether this citation is from an outside source is impossible. One reason for this is that there is no introductory formula prior to the verse. Up to this point the use of a formula has been Peter's method for signaling a citation. Furthermore, vv. 22-24 all begin with the relative pronoun ὅς, for which Christ (v. 21) is the antecedent. From this similar construction one cannot determine which verse—or whether all the verses—are coming from a cited text. A second possible citation comes in 3:10-12. The Greek text indicates this is a citation, but the only introduction to these verses is the singular word γὰρ.[39] If 3:10-12 is a citation, it would be the longest one thus far in the epistle. Again, while these two portions of the second body section could contain citations, it is not possible to determine from the literary context.

The concept of people's identities as transient strangers and resident aliens is becoming increasingly important in the universe of discourse. The two terms the author has used to describe his audience are now connected to specific ethical commands. The world that is portrayed here indicates that there may be some issues with submission, both to fellow believers and to those in positions of authority in the world. Peter's advice is to be submissive, to honor all men, and to love the brotherhood. Moreover, the admonitions are prompted by a concern for their souls due to the raging war that is taking place between them and their sinful desires (2:11).

---

39. While the conjunction γὰρ would not necessarily confirm that these verses are not a citation—since Peter varies in his use of introductory formulas—this conjunction occurs ten times in 1 Peter. To label 3:10-12 as a citation would require developing criteria for determining which occurrences of γὰρ signal citations. Contrasted with this is the use of the conjunction διότι in 1 Peter. The latter occurs only three times, and each time it appears as an introduction to a citation (see the First Body Section).

Defending Hope

Third Body Section (3:13—4:11)

Suffering emerges as the main topic addressed in the third section of the body. Five out of twelve total occurrences of πάσχω (and related verbal forms) appear in this section (cf. 3:14, 17, 18; 4:1 [2]). The governing ethical maxim offered is "it is better to suffer for doing good rather than for doing evil" (3:17; cf. 2:20). The approach taken by Peter is similar to that in 2:21–25. In both cases, Christ is offered as an example of how to conduct oneself in the midst of suffering, which is followed then by specific illustrations from his life. Christ's obedience in suffering went as far as the point of death (2:24; 3:18), but he was made alive by the Spirit and was resurrected (3:18, 21). In 4:2, Peter returns to the admonition of 2:11 (abstaining from sinful desires) in order that he might demonstrate that even in a state of suffering one is able to live for God's will rather than be entrenched in sinful desires.

An eschatological tone is struck in 4:7. The nearness of the end (πάντων δὲ τὸ τέλος ἤγγικεν) is followed with two imperative commands to be of sound mind (σωφρονήσατε) and to be self-controlled (νήψατε). Although the end is near, submitting to societal pressures or sinful desires is not warranted; rather, the end emphasizes all the more the holy behavior to which they are called. The purpose of this instruction is so that, through Jesus, God may be praised, honored, and glorified (4:11). The doxology which concludes this section of the body ties directly back to the reason for their trials: "in order that the testing of your faith [via the trials] . . . may be found to result in praise, glory, and honor at the revelation of Jesus Christ" (1:7). Therefore, the third body section adds to the universe of discourse a heightened sense of urgency on the part of the audience to live holy and Godly lives.

Forth Body Section (4:12—5:11)

The fourth and final section of the body is marked by the second occurrence of the plural vocative address ἀγαπητοί. The topic of suffering is treated once more in 4:12–19; this text can be viewed as the first subsection. Peter calls on the people to rejoice (χαίρετε, 4:13) in their circumstance of suffering, a point that supplements their rejoicing in the work of God and Christ in salvation (cf. 1:3–6a). The ethical maxim that characterized the second and third body sections also is found in this final section. Additionally, the household imagery is brought forward once again, but this time in reference to God's house (τοῦ οἴκου τοῦ θεοῦ, 4:17) as the initial object of God's judgment. The latter statement, however, is not set forth as a means of intimidation, but as a reminder that God also will judge the ones responsible for causing their suffering ("And if it [judgment] begins with us, what will be the end of those who are disobedient to the gospel of God?" [4:17]). At the close of this subsection, the Greek text denotes v. 18 as a citation. While this would fit Peter's method for citing at the end of section to corroborate his point, the textual marker (καὶ, a common conjunction) does not lend toward this conclusion.

Three groups of people are addressed specifically in the second subsection (5:1–11): elders (πρεσβυτέρους, 5:1), younger ones (νεώτεροι, 5:5a), and all of them (πάντες, 5:5b). The appeal to the elders echoes elements from the passage addressed to slaves in 2:18–25. They are instructed to be shepherds (5:2; cf. 2:25) of God's flock and examples (5:3; cf. 2:21) to them as well. Submission to the elders is the sole commandment directed to the young ones (5:5a). Finally, five imperative commands are directed to the whole group in just five short verses (5:5–9). The final instance of a cited text in 1 Peter is marked in the Greek text at v. 5. As with the supposed citation in 4:18, the textual marker is the lone conjunction ὅτι, which also is a very common conjunction.

An examination of the body proper (1:3—5:11) reveals a similar beginning and ending to the body. The conceptual inclusio that brackets this larger section highlights the temporary nature of the audience's suffering. In 1:6, the situation of suffering is described as ὀλίγον ἄρτι εἰ δέον ἐστὶν λυπηθέντες ἐν ποικίλοις πειρασμοῖς, whereas in 5:10 it is simply ὀλίγον παθόντας. In both contexts, there is an appeal to what God had done for them (1:3–5; 5:10) and to the hope and glory of Christ (1:3, 7; 5:10). Therefore, the inclusio communicates that there is cause for rejoicing and hope in the midst of this difficult circumstance. A semantic analysis reveals the body proper is bracketed by the controlling image of *hope in suffering*.

Postscript (5:12–14)

Peter's Epistle to the elect strangers of the diaspora closes with final greetings (from "she who is in Babylon" and "my son Mark") and two final commands ("stand" in God's grace and "greet" one another). Much has been made of the enigmatic phrase ἡ ἐν Βαβυλῶνι. Most commentators take this phrase to be a veiled reference to the church in Rome. Moreover, many argue that this word is the counterpart to διασπορᾶς in 1:1, with both words referring to a place that is not one's home. At the intratextual level, however, none of these connections are viable because they require one to access encyclopedic knowledge. A connection between the postscript and prescript that can be substantiated at the level of the universe of discourse pertains to the description of ἡ ἐν Βαβυλῶνι as συνεκλεκτὴ ("chosen together/with"). The latter echoes the description of the letter's recipients as ἐκλεκτοῖς (1:1). Regardless of the identity of the referent for "she who is in Babylon," the emphasis is on her being chosen as well. Finally, and as in the prescript, Peter appeals to χάρις (5:12) and εἰρήνη (5:14). In conclusion, an examination of the postscript reveals that the entire epistle is bracketed by the themes of election, grace, and peace. When combined with the theme of *hope in suffering* in the body, the author makes explicit the framework in which he will incorporate references from other texts.

Summary

A semantic analysis of 1 Peter reveals many essential features of the universe of discourse of the document. When the signs are examined in relation to one another and in relation to the syntactic structure, key assumptions about the world and reality become apparent. The prescript of the epistle initiates the reading contract between author and reader by revealing a world in which both parties are connected through Jesus Christ. Concepts which recur in this universe are introduced here as well: election (1:1; 2:4, 6, 9; 5:13), strangers (1:1, 17; 2:11), household imagery (1:2, 3, 23; 2:2, 4–10; 4:17; 5:12), grace (1:10, 13; 2:19–20; 3:7; 4:10; 5:5, 10), and peace (1:2; 5:14). When the postscript is viewed together with the prescript, the universe of discourse appears to be bracketed by the themes of election, grace, and peace. The prescript also suggests this universe is one in which God, Jesus, and the Spirit are active in the world and are central to the identity of the recipients.

The introduction reveals the reality of suffering/trials for both the recipients (1:6) and for Jesus (1:11). Suffering resurfaces numerous times and is one of the main issues addressed throughout the epistle (2:19–21, 23; 3:14, 17–18; 4:1, 15, 19; 5:10). Moreover, the recipients' situation is given further description as a raging war between them and two competing fronts: their evil desires (2:11) and their adversary the devil (5:8).[40] While

---

40. Interestingly, in at least three places in 1 Peter the author exhorts his audience to take certain actions by using metaphorical language that would indicate either

their situation might seem hopeless, the author draws on another reality that serves as a positive reminder: their salvation (1:5, 6, 9, 10). Precisely because they enjoy this status before God they are called to be submissive (2:13, 18; 3:1; 5:5). The eschatological remarks in the epistle add to this situation a sense of urgency (2:12; 4:7, 17). The coupling of election, grace, and peace (prescript and postscript) with God's salvation and provision (the inclusio of the body proper) gives substance to the syntactic structure and creates the context for the author's ethical exhortations. As a result, the audience can find comfort in their status before God and hope despite their trying circumstances.

Finally, a semantic analysis assists in determining references to other texts. The main criterion for identifying citations at the intratextual level is the presence of some sort of textual marker or formula. In 1 Peter, the author uses a variety of formulas to introduce a citation from another text: (διότι γέγραπται, διότι, and διότι περιέχει ἐν γραφῇ). The intertextual references are found in 1:16; 1:24–25; and 2:6. Peter's use of these references typically provides corroborating evidence for both the ethical exhortations to his audience and the discussion of their identity as the people of God. The references are placed strategically at the end of a discourse section before a transition to the next topic. While other places may exist in 1 Peter where textual citations are present, identifying these occurrences would go beyond the borders of the universe of discourse.

Pragmatics

The final step of an intratextual investigation is an analysis of the relationship between signs and their users (or texts and their readers). Alkier described this step as involving a determination of the ideology of the text. What are the practical or pragmatic effects of the signs when read as they appear in the text? Another way to approach this step is to ask the question, how should 1 Peter be read? Thus, what themes, motifs, ideas, beliefs, convictions, et cetera form the backdrop for a reading of this epistle?[41]

---

preparation for battle (1:13, "having girded the loins of your mind"; 4:1, "arm yourselves with the same attitude") or preparation by being properly clothed (5:5, "clothe yourselves with humility").

41. Cf. Alkier, "Intertextuality," 14–15. Here his text-pragmatic analysis of Mark's Gospel leads him to the conclusion that the Markan parable chapter (Mark 4) provides "the proper theme for an adequate reading of Mark's Gospel." This theme is none other than the choice of "whether to be inside or outside, in conjunction or disjunction, with

Defending Hope

As with the previous two steps in this investigation, a pragmatic analysis must also be shielded from any form of encyclopedic knowledge, especially one's own. Therefore, not every question that surfaces will be answerable on the intratextual level. Many of these questions will be carried over into the intertextual investigation.

In order to properly analyze the pragmatic effects of the linguistic signs in 1 Peter, this final step of the intratextual investigation aims to provide a lens through which the epistle should be read. First, the major themes discovered through the semantic analysis will be examined on a broader level by assessing the worldview communicated by the author. Attention here will be given to the role of stories in communicating the theological and ethical components of the epistle and how these stories shed light on the author's purpose. Then the pragmatic lens for reading 1 Peter will be provided. Examining these aspects of 1 Peter will assist in answering the primary question in view, how should 1 Peter be read?

Worldview and Implied Narrative

In 1 Peter, nothing less than an intricate theological worldview is painted. The author uses theological truths to shape his audience's thinking about the world and their behavior in the world.[42] Instruction and command presuppose a specific theological understanding. In other words, the author's construction of the universe of discourse is done in such a way that morality, rooted in theological truth, is of utmost importance. J. de Waal Dryden described the author's method as follows: "Before giving them moral instructions, he gives them a moral vision that places them within a moral universe. He does this by depicting not simply a theological worldview, but a *narrative* theological worldview."[43] The concept of worldview is helpful here because it provides a proper framework in which the major themes of 1 Peter can be examined. Two terms mentioned by Dryden require further explication: *worldview* and *narrative*.

---

the values of the Gospel, in discipleship to Jesus, or on the way to judgment."

42. For an excellent study on the theology and ethics of 1 Peter, see Dryden, *Theology and Ethics*. Dryden describes his work as an analysis of "the pragmatics of theological discourse in 1 Peter" (12). While his method of examining the epistle is based on concepts from rhetorical and social-scientific approaches, Dryden states that his methodological eclecticism is influenced primarily by the tenets of discourse analysis and speech-act theory.

43. Dryden, *Theology and Ethics*, 64.

The Textual Universe of 1 Peter

Worldview is defined most broadly as "the grid through which humans perceive reality."[44] According to N. T. Wright, this grid includes elements such as stories, symbols, praxis, and questions. Moreover, Dryden added that worldviews consist of both intellectual and cultural elements, both physical and non-physical. As a result, worldviews provide "an all-encompassing picture of reality touching all spheres of human knowledge and activity that serves to integrate human existence into a comprehensible unity."[45] Functionally, worldviews are normative in force due to the claim they make on reality. Individuals adopting a specific worldview not only have a lens through which to view reality, but they also find legitimization and significance for their own actions within the world. Worldviews bring together all these elements and ascribe meaning to every aspect of life.

If worldview consists of both physical and non-physical elements, then this necessitates drawing upon encyclopedic knowledge at some point in the reconstruction process. Thus, the description provided in this section provides only a partial (or limited) reconstruction of the worldview as presented by the text of 1 Peter. Physical elements such as architecture, artifacts, and clothing will not be examined here since these elements go beyond the borders of the text and its universe. At this point, the second of Dryden's two terms assists in keeping one within the bounds of the universe of discourse.

Narrative is "that work which renders experience significant, humanly meaningful."[46] Narratives have elements such as plot, characters, and setting and are taken by many to be synonymous with *story*.[47] Perhaps the most effective way in which a worldview is communicated is through a narrative or story, whether oral or written. In defining worldview, Wright also indicated his belief that worldviews have "an irreducible narrative element."[48] His conviction is that stories are a primary characteristic of worldviews, so much so that they operate at a more fundamental level than one's stated beliefs. Stories can communicate world origins, cultural values,

---

44. Wright, *The People of God*, 38.

45. Dryden, *Theology and Ethics*, 55.

46. Loughlin, *Telling God's Story*, 139. His definition is based on that of Paul Ricoeur.

47. While distinctions are made between *narrative* and *story*, holding to these distinctions is not necessary for a pragmatic approach to 1 Peter. The two terms are used interchangeably here. For a synopsis of the distinctions between narrative and story, see Loughlin, *Telling God's Story*, 52–63.

48. Wright, *The People of God*, 38.

Defending Hope

and core beliefs. Moreover, since worldviews claim a specific view of reality, the stories that characterize them often can come into conflict.

Dryden argues that stories can be used to portray all of reality as a meta-narrative. This meta-narrative or *narrative worldview*, as he terms it, is defined as a construct that "communicates a worldview in a concrete form as a realized picture of reality, not simply a set of ideas. Additionally it *shows* the relationships of different persons and realities within the worldview, instead of having to define them abstractly."[49] Dryden's combination of the two terms (*narrative* and *worldview*) is not new; others refer to this concept as a *narrative universe*.[50] A narrative worldview not only gives meaning to its adherents, it also presents and reinforces moral behavior.

At this point two pragmatic questions surface that must be answered: Does 1 Peter tell a story? If so, what does this story communicate concerning meaning and moral direction? Technically, 1 Peter is not narrative in genre, but it exhibits a *narrative substructure* that presents the story in terms of both realities and sequential events.[51] The narrative substructure governs the epistle, and it is this structure that points to a presupposed narrative world.

In his commentary on 1 Peter, M. Eugene Boring described the situation as it pertains to the audience: "The author places their experience within the framework of the real world . . . by addressing them from within this world, confirming the new world they received at their new birth, and by deepening and widening their perception of the new reality in which they live."[52] Through the semantic analysis it was discovered that references to salvation are central to the epistle, though these references may be only smaller pieces of the larger salvation story. Since the narrative world is understood and accepted by the audience, not every facet necessitates delineation. The pieces of the story of God's salvation included in 1 Peter, especially those found in the introduction (1:3–12), point to the implied narrative

---

49. Dryden, *Theology and Ethics*, 56. Moreover, he claims that "narrative worldviews are able to communicate beliefs and ethos together, and for this reason are often more effective than doctrinal abstractions" (56).

50. For the use of *narrative universe*, see Wilson, *The Hope of Glory*. Dryden, in his discussion of worldview, drew heavily upon Wilson's work.

51. See Dryden, *Theology and Ethics*, 66, though he is borrowing the term from Hays, *The Faith*.

52. Boring, *1 Peter*, 184. His appendix entitled "The Narrative World of 1 Peter" (183–201) is extremely insightful. In this appendix, Boring identified and classified 157 *events* that comprise the narrative world of 1 Peter.

of this larger context. Therefore, based on the material introduced in the prescript and frequently mentioned throughout the epistle, 1 Peter does narrate a story, a story of God's salvation. The latter would then provide a lens through which the audience must interpret their present suffering.

In regard to the second question, the story of God's salvation as it appears in 1 Peter must communicate something about meaning and moral direction. At the outset, it is imperative to understand that the story of the audience is presented within the story of God's salvation. The prescript and introduction to the epistle begin by narrating the story of the audience—a story of strangers and their suffering in this world—and how their story fits into the larger story of God's salvation, a story of election and salvation. Though the people are strangers in this world, they can rejoice and hope in the fact of their election. Though they grieve due to difficult trials, they can take comfort in the fact of their salvation. Thus, the story of God's salvation throughout history is the context both for the audience's own story and for their interpretation of their present circumstances. Peter's masterful intertwining of these two stories culminates in a message of hope for his audience, as figure 2 illustrates below.

Figure 2. Story and Hope in 1 Peter

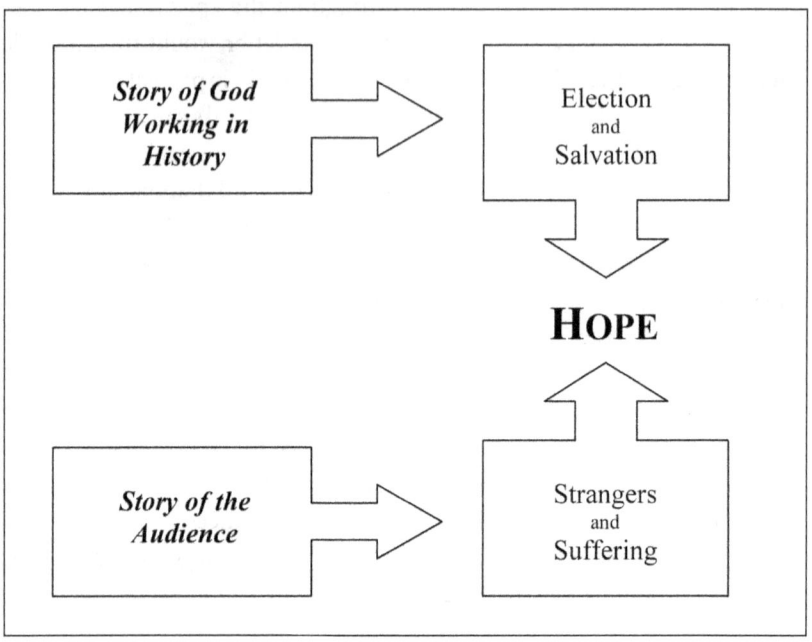

From the beginning of the epistle, hope emerges as a primary theme for understanding 1 Peter. The weaving together of the two stories achieves two results: (1) a story of hope is narrated, and (2) the audience is placed meaningfully within the narrative worldview.[53] From this the author proceeds to interpret their current context through the lens of these two stories by offering ethical exhortations for their specific set of trials. Thus, moral instruction comprises the majority of material that follows in the major sections of the epistle.

The function of the implied narrative worldview of 1 Peter is, as Dryden stated, "to contextualize ethics by picturing a universe in which the epistle's instructions are reasonable and significant."[54] Not only does 1 Peter narrate a story of hope, but it also communicates the expected behavior of God's people even in trying circumstances. The epistle embodies a unique blend of indicative and imperative. In other words, just as the

---

53. As Dryden stated, "He [the author] is mapping their life experiences directly onto the grand narrative of salvation, from creation to eschaton, and thus placing their lives (personal and corporate) within the context of an overarching narrative worldview" (*Theology and Ethics*, 68).

54. Dryden, *Theology and Ethics*, 81–82.

stories of God's salvation and the audience's suffering are intertwined, so also are the epistle's statements on theology and ethics. Consequently, one might expect the intertextual references to OT Scripture in 1 Peter either to demonstrate further the hope believers can have despite their circumstances or to support a specific word of moral exhortation.

A Pragmatic Lens for Reading 1 Peter

The question posed at the outset of this subsection was, what are the practical or pragmatic effects of the signs when read as they appear in the text? One pragmatic effect is that the signs present the reader with a portrait of how God has worked in history and how he currently works in the lives of his people. A further pragmatic effect is the sense of hope offered when one views the audience's story as part of the larger story of salvation history. The intertwining of these two stories is set forth in the prescript, and its practical implications are laid bare in the rest of the epistle. Accordingly, a pragmatic analysis reveals the purpose of the composition of 1 Peter, that is, to offer a word of hope and exhortation to a struggling community of believers who are to be set apart in the world.

So, how should 1 Peter be read? If the implied narrative worldview provides the backdrop for 1 Peter, then the epistle should be read through the lens of hope (1:3). While other recurring themes are present—such as grace (in suffering [2:19, 20; 5:10] and in salvation [1:2, 10, 13; 4:10; 5:5, 10]) and election—hope is the primary thrust of the theological and ethical statements in the epistle. The stories of God's salvation and the audience's suffering are woven together to form a tight-knit cord that permeates every section of the epistle. Therefore, hope gathers together all the other major images and themes in 1 Peter and is an appropriate interpretive lens through which the epistle's content should be read.

Summary: The Universe of Discourse of 1 Peter

What does the universe of 1 Peter encompass? What world is projected by the text of the epistle? In what ways can this world be ordered and described? What views about the world and reality must author and reader hold in common for the signs to communicate? By examining the syntactic, semantic, and pragmatic elements of the epistle, the universe of discourse of 1 Peter can be reconstructed and answers to these questions can be supplied.

Defending Hope

First, the syntactic analysis revealed that the universe of discourse has a distinct structure within which the signs operate. An epistolary approach to the structure of 1 Peter presents a fairly agreed-upon division of the epistle that delineates a prescript, postscript, introduction, and three main sections (with some variation). A rhetorical approach to the structure of the epistle has similar divisions, but most of the variation with this approach comes with the section from 2:11 to 5:11. Based on syntactical insights from both approaches, a syntactic structure was adopted for the text's universe. In this analysis, the utilization of two different approaches to a text's structure demonstrates how a semiotic method for studying texts also allows for the incorporation of varying methodologies.

Second, an examination of the signs within the framework of the syntactic structure revealed many essential features of the text's universe of discourse. The opening of this universe is initiated by the epistolary prescript. Election, grace, and peace emerge as themes in the prescript, and these themes are reiterated in the postscript. The prescript also portrays a world in which God, Jesus, and the Spirit are always at work. Both the prescript and the introduction describe the situation of the audience, on the one hand, as those who are strangers suffering difficult trials. On the other hand, their hopeless situation is infused with hope by the reminder of their salvation and its positive benefits. The themes that bracket the whole of 1 Peter give substance to the syntactic structure and create the context for the ethical instruction in the major sections of the epistle's body. Additionally, the semantic analysis revealed some recurring formulas for the author's introduction of external citations.

Third, the pragmatic analysis allowed for the incorporation of *worldview*—and its constitutive element of *story*—to determine the practical effects when one reads the signs of 1 Peter. The worldview of 1 Peter is composed of two intertwined stories: the story of salvation history and the story of the audience. The two stories are introduced in the prescript, expounded upon in the introduction, and interpreted throughout the body of the epistle. As a result, the message presented by the weaving together of the stories is one of *hope*. The worldview presented by 1 Peter drives not only the ethical exhortations, but also the statements on the identity of the audience. Thus, the linguistic signs in 1 Peter are read appropriately through the lens of hope.

Finally, an intratextual investigation permits one to draw conclusions on how external or intertextual references might be used. First, as one approaches the intertextual references in 1 Peter, one should expect these linguistic signs to be consistent with the universe of discourse set forth in the epistle. Thus, it would be reasonable to expect the intertextual references to cohere with the message of hope that is central to the epistle. Second, the very fact that the author references such texts implies not only the reader's presumed knowledge of the texts, but also the authority of the text for both author and reader. Third, the semantic analysis revealed the use of different formulas for introducing external citations. When encyclopedic knowledge is accessed in the intertextual analysis, this information may possibly disclose other methods for introducing citations, specifically references to the OT.

4

Opening the Encyclopedia of 1 Peter

INTERTEXTUALITY IS CONCERNED WITH the relationships between a text and other texts. An intertextual perspective builds upon an intratextual investigation, but moves beyond the text's universe to the level of encyclopedic knowledge. Before examining the Isaianic references in detail, however, I will address in this chapter the following preliminary issues that allow us to "open" the encyclopedia of 1 Peter: historical and social concerns, textual tradition, and citation practices. Knowledge of these items will assist in properly contextualizing the analyses of the intertextual references.

The matter of which encyclopedia to use when examining a text has been discussed in chapter 2. Following the conclusion reached there, a prudent approach is to study the intertextual references through the encyclopedia in force at the time of the composition of 1 Peter. Nonetheless, intertextual references present a unique situation in regard to the choice of encyclopedia. Does one interpret the references based on the encyclopedia in force at the time they were incorporated into another text, or does one interpret these references based on the encyclopedia in force at the time the references themselves were first written? In other words, should the Isaianic references in 1 Peter be interpreted based on a first-century A.D. Christian encyclopedia or an eighth-century B.C. Jewish encyclopedia or both?[1] Adhering to Eco's understanding of the role of an encyclopedia re-

---

1. The author is aware of the historical issues surrounding the dating of Isaiah's composition and the events it narrates. The eighth century B.C. is used here to reflect the view that the book of Isaiah was penned by Isaiah himself. One easily can insert any other century reflecting another position on the dating of Isaiah and still have the intended contrast.

quires that only the first-century A.D. Christian encyclopedia, in this case, be used as the basis for interpreting the Isaianic references.

On the other hand, Alkier's work on miracles in the Pauline Epistles demonstrates that the encyclopedia of Judaism is incorporated into Paul's letters specifically through the use of intertextual references. Therefore, intertextual study would carry with it at least some preconception of this body of documents and its encyclopedic context. Correspondingly, Huizenga stated that when the NT was written, the OT existed only as it was remembered, written, and interpreted in Jewish culture. He then offered the following plea for those doing intertextual studies: "Historical investigation into the New Testament use of the Old Testament thus requires us to move beyond the Old Testament itself as a pure ideal. . . . Scholars must ask how Old Testament texts were actually understood within Jewish culture when the New Testament documents were written."[2] Huizenga's comments certainly warrant reflection in light of the lack of a fixed canon of OT Scripture. His statements point to an often-debated issue in intertextual studies: What aspects of the NT writers' exegetical methods and interpretive conclusions are descriptive and what aspects are normative? Hopefully, the intertextual investigation in chapter 5 will shed light on this issue—at least in regard to the First Epistle of Peter—by allowing the first-century Christian encyclopedia proper interaction with its Jewish encyclopedia.

In light of the comments above, I will focus on the relevant portions of the encyclopedia of first-century Christianity from which 1 Peter originated.[3] One also should bear in mind that the examination of the intertextual references to Isaiah is not a separate venture. Both the intertextual investigation and a discussion of selected encyclopedic elements will contribute to a greater comprehension of the wider encyclopedia of 1 Peter. Alkier stated that "each act of sign production and sign reception must be related to at least one encyclopedia of culturally conventionalized knowledge."[4] Part of reconstructing the culturally conventionalized knowledge requires a statement of the historical and cultural context for the composition of 1 Peter. Therefore, the first part of this section will

---

2. Huizenga, "The Matthean Jesus," 65.

3. The goal here is not to describe the virtual encyclopedia of first-century Christianity in its entirety. To do so would both go beyond the scope of this study and require an extensive examination of the other NT documents as well. This limitation is acknowledged by Alkier in his discussion of the encyclopedia (*Wunder und Wirklichkeit*, 285).

4. Alkier, "New Testament Studies," 233.

provide summary statements on some of the key historical and social issues that will form the backdrop for the intertextual analysis.

A further description of the encyclopedia that Alkier offered is as follows: "An encyclopedia consists not only of linguistic knowledge but also of the knowledge of forms of address, norms of behavior, technical and practical knowledge, and so forth."[5] Part of the first-century Christian encyclopedia that is particularly relevant to an intertextual examination is both the texts that are referenced and how they are referenced. Thus, a treatment of the OT textual tradition followed by the NT authors and the citation practices is necessary.[6] A brief survey of all three issues (historical and social context, textual tradition, and citation practices) will allow for an approximate concretization of the *virtual* encyclopedia that will govern the examination of the intertextual references to Isaiah. The insights gleaned will complement the findings of the intratextual analysis in the previous chapter, and together the insights from both the encyclopedia and the universe of discourse will provide a framework for examining the Isaianic references.

Historical and Social Concerns

If signs are created for communicative purposes (Augustine) and if they are understood properly by examining them through the encyclopedia in force at their creation (Eco), then a semiotic investigation of Isaianic signs in 1 Peter necessitates knowledge of pertinent historical and cultural issues surrounding the composition of 1 Peter. While the broad range of such issues is covered in most commentaries, the present discussion will be limited to the following: authorship, recipients, date, and social and historical setting.[7] The goal here is to present a concise portrait of the historical land-

---

5. Ibid.

6. The author is aware of the issues involving the exact form of the canon of Scripture that existed during the time of the writing of the NT; however, this topic is not one that will be addressed in this study. The book of Isaiah—the only OT book examined in this study—is present in the earliest canon lists. Thus, only the methods used to cite this book, not its canonical status, need establishment. An excellent summary of the canon issue is offered by McLay, "Biblical Texts," 38–58. For more detailed works see Beckwith, *Old Testament Canon*; Ellis, *The Old Testament*; and McDonald and Sanders, *The Canon Debate*.

7. A detailed presentation of all the critical introductory issues will not be undertaken here. To do so would go well beyond the scope and purpose of this study.

scape of 1 Peter which will function as the reference point for determining the meaning of the signs.

The two issues of date and authorship are so connected that they must be examined together. Prior to the nineteenth century, Petrine authorship was not debated in the history of the church. Only recently has this fundamental assumption been challenged. Thus, there are two main camps regarding authorship: apostolic and pseudonymous.[8] The pseudonymous camp holds that Peter, the apostle, could not have written the epistle primarily because (1) the Greek is too good for a Galilean fisherman; (2) the author exhibits dependence on the deutero-Paulines; (3) the portrait of church structure and social hostility reflects a time later than Peter; and (4) the spread of Christianity to the named regions in 1:1 could not have happened until after Peter's lifetime.[9] The conclusion is that an anonymous author (with unknown motives) wrote in Peter's name after Peter's death. For these reasons, proponents of pseudonymous authorship would argue that the date of 1 Peter's composition was sometime between A.D. 70 and 90.

The apostolic camp takes the claim in 1:1 (Πέτρος ἀπόστολος Ἰησοῦ Χριστοῦ) prima facie. The author's reference to being "a witness of the sufferings of Christ" (5:1) and allusions to the teachings of Jesus corroborate this position.[10] Also, the social hostility portrayed in the epistle need not reflect an official, imperial persecution. On the contrary, 1 Peter encourages submission to governors (2:13) and honoring the emperor (2:17). As for the level of Greek in the epistle, an analysis of the letter's syntax arguably reveals that the author was Semitic and that Greek was his second language.[11] Therefore, those in the apostolic camp would argue that the

---

Therefore, opposing viewpoints, debated issues, and pertinent sources will be referenced in footnotes where appropriate.

8. A third position—and one I would subsume under the apostolic view—emphasizes the role of Silvanus (5:12) as the amanuensis for Peter. Under this view the writing of the epistle is placed either prior to Peter's death or soon after. Much of this survey on authorship is adapted from the fine treatment of this topic provided by Karen Jobes. See her commentary *1 Peter*, 5–19.

9. Tradition holds that the apostle Peter was martyred in Rome in the mid-60s under the Roman emperor Nero, and this viewpoint is virtually unanimous today. Points 2–4 all reflect a historical situation beyond the mid-60s.

10. On the allusions to the sayings of Jesus, see Selwyn's seminal work on the *verba Christi* in *St. Peter*, 23–24. Also see Gundry, "'Verba Christi,'" 336–50; and Wong, "Jesus' Sayings."

11. As Jobes, *1 Peter*, 6–8, argues sufficiently. On the syntax of 1 Peter she comments as follows: "This is perhaps the most telling feature of the Greek of 1 Peter, for a letter's

date of the epistle was shortly before the death of Peter in the early 60s. A Petrine authorship is held for the present study.

At the outset of 1 Peter, the audience is described as ἐκλεκτοῖς παρεπιδήμοις διασπορᾶς ("to the elect strangers of the diaspora," 1:1). This description indicates generally their identity (as elect strangers) and their location (in the diaspora). The former was described in the intratextual investigation as a paradoxical situation highlighting both a positive vertical dimension (elect before God) and a negative horizontal dimension (strangers in society). In 2:11, the author also calls the recipients πάροικοι ("resident aliens"). Taken together, παρεπιδήμοις and πάροικοι seem to describe the social situation of the audience as one of estrangement.[12] Most of current scholarship holds that these terms should not be understood literally but metaphorically as foreigners and aliens living away from the promised land. The general argument for the metaphorical view is that the terms used to describe the audience (1:1; 2:9-10, 11) are those terms used in the LXX of God's people and the historical situations in which they found themselves.[13]

The other major aspect of the audience that is debated is whether they were Christians of Jewish or Gentile origin. On the one hand, the geographical location of the diaspora is made more specific in 1:1 with the naming of select regions from Asia Minor (Pontus, Galatia, Cappadocia, Asia, and Bithynia).[14] If the term *diaspora* is taken literally, then this would require the audience to be primarily, if not exclusively, Jewish. Indeed, the presence

---

syntax flows almost subconsciously from an author's proficiency with the language, unlike the deliberate structure, content, and ornamentation of a discourse" (7). See also her excursus, "The Syntax of 1 Peter: How Good Is the Greek?" 325-38.

12. This position is argued vehemently by Elliott. See *A Home*; and idem, *1 Peter*. See also the discussion of these terms in chapter 3 of this book.

13. In the LXX, see Gen 15:13; 23:4; Exod 2:22; Lev 25:23; Deut 23:8; 1 Chr 29:15; Ps 38:13; 104:12-13; and 118:19. In his discussion of παρεπιδήμοις and πάροικοι, Achtemeier supplies another convincing reason for the metaphorical position: "The fact that the phrase in 2:11 is introduced with ὡς, a particle regularly used in 1 Peter to identify a metaphorical word or phrase, points rather to a metaphorical than a literal intention of the two concepts, and the situation presumed in such verses as 4:3-4 indicates rather a reduction of social acceptance than a failure to increase it as a result of becoming Christian. It is therefore unlikely that one can deduce anything about the prior political status of the readers by the use of these terms in 1 Peter" (*1 Peter*, 56).

14. In the previous intratextual investigation, the universe of discourse did not allow for an examination of these geographical areas. When encyclopedic knowledge is accessed, however, one can examine these regions and give a precise description of the term *diaspora*.

of a sizable Jewish population in first-century Asia Minor makes this view plausible.[15] On the other hand, internal evidence in the epistle points to a Gentile background. Three statements referring to the audience's identity are of note: (1) 1:18: "you were redeemed from your empty way of life handed down by your forefathers"; (2) 2:10: "once you were not a people, but now you are the people of God"; and (3) 4:3: a vice list containing items that would not characterize Jews. The argument is that none of these statements would have been used to describe diaspora Jews and their former way of life.[16] For this study, the recipients are viewed as metaphorical exiles who are predominantly Gentile.

The final historical/cultural issue is that of the epistle's setting. Aspects of the historical setting already have been intimated in the discussions of authorship, date, and audience above. In short, the occasion or context of 1 Peter is suffering.[17] Various references to the suffering, grief, and trials of the audience are found in 1 Peter (e.g., 1:6; 2:18–21; 3:9, 13–14, 17; 4:1, 12–16, 19; 5:9–10). While the exact nature of this suffering is difficult to identify precisely, it is likely that this sort of suffering was a localized form of persecution. Prior to the 1970s, the dominant view of the historical setting of 1 Peter was an official Roman persecution. Robert Webb offered three reasons for the increasing rejection of this view by Petrine scholars: (1) historical evidence for an official persecution during the time of composition is lacking; (2) the texts referring to suffering are better interpreted as involving informal suffering; and (3) the source of suffering is never identified as the Roman government.[18] Webb concluded that the situation can be described as one of "slander and verbal abuse intended to demean and discredit them (with the possibility of physical abuse in household social relationships)."[19] The view of the historical setting adopted for this study follows the latter interpretation.

---

15. For more on this issue, see Trebilco, *Jewish*, 32.

16. Jobes argues, however, that the spiritually bankrupt way of life actually would have characterized both Jews and Gentiles. Thus, "it makes little difference whether the original readers were Jews or Gentiles. . . . Whether Peter's readers were formerly Jews or Gentiles, Peter addresses them indiscriminately from within the traditions of biblical Israel, in which the author was thoroughly steeped" (*1 Peter*, 24).

17. See the helpful excursus on suffering ("Suffering in 1 Peter and the New Testament") offered by Davids in *First Epistle of Peter*, 30–44.

18. Webb, "The Petrine Epistles," 382.

19. Ibid., 383.

Defending Hope

Textual Tradition and Citation Practices

The second preliminary issue concerns tendencies in textual tradition when the NT authors cited OT Scripture. The goal here is to determine which texts and versions were available to the NT writers and which versions they likely would have utilized as well. The writings contained in the OT were originally composed in Hebrew with some portions in Aramaic.[20] The critical edition of the Hebrew text used today, referred to as the Masoretic Text (MT), does not date as far back as the first century A.D.; however, comparative studies between this critical text and texts found at Qumran have demonstrated that the MT is an accurate version of the text that circulated in the first century.[21] In the first century A.D., however, OT Scripture circulated in Greek, Latin, and Aramaic as well. Furthermore, each of these existed in several versions.[22]

Of the aforementioned versions, the best-known Greek translation, the Septuagint (LXX), is the one most often quoted by the NT writers. In many ways, though, the term *Septuagint* is a misnomer in that it implies a level of unity or homogeneity that is not present. The reality is that numerous authors composed it at different times and in different places.[23] The books of the Pentateuch were translated into Greek first, *ca.* 250 B.C., with the remaining portions of the OT translated in the following two centuries. Subsequently, the Greek OT text underwent multiple revisions and translations. All of these issues require scholars to be precise when using a term such as *Septuagint*. Thus, Jobes and Silva argue that "it is probably better to refer to the original translation of books other than the Pentateuch as the

---

20. The Aramaic portions are found in Gen 31:47; Jer 10:11; Dan 2:4—7:28; Ezra 4:8—6:18; and 7:12–26.

21. In his summary of the pre-masoretic period, Mulder states, "What we now call the 'masoretic text' appears to have been a Hebrew text which was authoritative in many respects and whose transmission was surrounded with great care in the Jewish world, even in sectarian groups, several centuries before the beginning of the Common Era" ("The Transmission," 104). See Mulder's full article for the significance of the Masoretes in the transmission and preservation of the OT text.

22. The multiformity of the biblical text is attested by findings at Qumran and the Dead Sea region (including proto-Masoretic, Samaritan, Septuagintal, and Aramaic Targumim) and the pseudepigraphal *Letter of Aristeas* (for the origin of the Greek version of the OT). Though scholars assume the inauthenticity of the *Letter of Aristeas*, it probably preserves some reliable information. For an argument for the latter, see Jobes and Silva, *Invitation to the Septuagint*, 34–37.

23. For a detailed but concise account of the history of the Septuagint, see ibid., 30–34.

Old Greek (OG) so as to distinguish them from the original translation of the Pentateuch and from the later revisions and new translations."[24] Since the present study examines only the use of Isaiah, the Greek text of the OT included for comparison in the following sections will be labeled "OG" following the suggestion of Jobes and Silva.

Since the NT was written and transmitted in Greek, the question for intertextual studies becomes apparent: Did the author quote directly from the LXX/OG, or did he translate (or even paraphrase) from the Hebrew text? In some instances, an intertextual reference might contain different words than both the LXX/OG and Hebrew, or it might seem that the text was changed deliberately. On the other hand, this variation could be due to the use of a different textual tradition to which scholars today do not have access. Craig Evans stated this problem succinctly: "What at first may appear to be an inaccurate quotation, or a quotation of the LXX, itself thought to be an inaccurate translation of the underlying Hebrew, may in fact be a quotation of a different textual tradition."[25] Recognition of the multiformity of the biblical text during this time makes assumptions about the inaccuracy of a citation conjectural at best.

The third issue to examine is the way in which OT texts were cited in the first century. Since the encyclopedia in view is distinctly Christian, it will suffice to examine the citation practices in the NT and any Jewish elements that were carried over into these practices. One common practice that usually indicates a direct citation is the use of an introductory formula.[26] An introductory formula is a word or group of words used to signal a textual citation. Introductory formulas can be either specific or general, and they usually precede the cited text, though sometimes the formula directly can follow the citation.[27]

The two most common formulas are the more generic γέγραπται (commonly preceded by καθὼς and οὕτως) and ἐστίν γεγραμμένον (or γεγραμμένον ἐστίν). Sometimes, general formulas are made more specific when accompanied by phrases indicating the source of the citation from OT Scripture or the name of an OT figure, such as the Law (ἐν τῷ νόμῳ, 1

---

24. Ibid., 32.

25. Evans, *From Prophecy*, 5.

26. The discussion here of introductory formulas is not exhaustive but cursory. Only a few passages are cited as an example of any one formula. For a more extensive treatment of these formulas, see Longenecker, *Biblical Exegesis*. Another helpful discussion, though dated, is Metzger, "The Formulas," 297–307.

27. E.g., John 1:23.

Cor 14:21; John 10:34; 15:25), the Prophets (ἐν τοῖς προφήταις, Acts 13:40; John 6:45), Moses (Μωϋσῆς, Rom 10:19; Mark 12:19; Luke 20:28), and Isaiah (Ἡσαΐας, Rom 10:16; Mark 1:2; John 12:39). Moreover, some formulas (ἵνα πληρωθῇ or ἵνα τελειωθῇ) are used to indicate the author's belief that an OT citation has reached its fulfillment in some way. Another way of referencing the OT is with ἡ γραφή ("the Scripture"). Often, this noun is utilized as an introductory formula when combined with ἵνα πληρωθῇ, ἵνα τελειωθῇ, λέγει, or περιέχει.

In some places in the NT, a direct citation of an OT text occurs, but with no introductory formula (e.g., Rom 11:34–35). The lack of such formulas in the most logical places has led some to argue for the use of *explicit markers* by the NT writers.[28] Explicit markers are common conjunctions and include words such as ὅτι, διότι, γάρ, and καί. An author might use one of these markers when a text is particularly well known and a formula would be superfluous. Also, an explicit marker is used to separate the references when a string of texts are cited together (Rom 9:25–26) and possibly to indicate a change in source text (Rom 15:10–11). The difficulty with these markers is that they are extremely common words in the NT; thus, not every occurrence will signal a citation.

Occasionally, an introductory formula will be present, but the following supposed citation will have no clear ties to a specific OT text. For instance, in John 7:38, Jesus uses an introductory formula (καθὼς εἶπεν ἡ γραφή) to introduce the statement, "From within him will flow rivers of living water." Scholars acknowledge the location of this referent text as a *crux interpretum* since it could be from Isa 58:11; Ps 40:8; Prov 18:4; or Zech 14:8. Also, in John 19:28, the author includes a formula (ἵνα τελειωθῇ ἡ γραφή) to indicate the fulfillment of Jesus's statement of thirst from the cross (Διψῶ). Like John 7:38, multiple possibilities are propounded as the source of this citation (namely, Ps 22:15 and Ps 69:21). Therefore, introductory formulas do not always guarantee the correct identification of the referent text.

In Second Temple Judaism, the above formulas also were used widely, especially to reinforce the authority of a citation.[29] E. Earle Ellis noted four examples of exegetical terminology found in the NT that reflects a distinc-

---

28. See Moyise and Menken, *Isaiah*, 175. The page reference is located in their chapter entitled "Isaiah in 1 Peter," which is particularly insightful for the present study.

29. As is demonstrated by Metzger, "The Formulas"; and Fitzmyer, "The Use," 299–305.

tively Jewish form of exegesis.[30] First, the formula πιστὸς ὁ λόγος ("faithful is the word") found in 1–2 Timothy and Titus reflects a phrase found in the Qumran *Book of Mysteries* that refers to a prophecy. Second, another Qumranic phrase carried over into the NT is οὗτος ἐστιν ("this is"). The latter formula is equivalent to the Qumran exegetical method of *pesher* and is used two ways: (1) to introduce a commentary that follows a cited text (Rom 9:7–9; Acts 2:16; John 6:31; Heb 7:5) or (2) to introduce an OT text to explain a previously narrated event (Matt 3:3; 11:10; Acts 4:11). Third, the adversatives ἀλλά and δέ ("but") are used frequently in the OT and NT both before and after citations either to introduce them or to qualify them, respectively. Finally, the verbs ἀκούειν ("hear") and μανθάνειν ("learn") are used occasionally in both rabbinic literature and the NT to reinforce the understanding of Scripture that is cited (Matt 9:13; 21:33; 24:32).

A cursory glance at the ways in which OT texts are referenced in the NT reveals some helpful parameters for examining the Isaianic citations in 1 Peter. Some references are specifically marked ("Isaiah says"), some are generally marked ("it is written" or "for"), and some are not marked. On the one hand, the frequency of occurrence of introductory formulas in the NT assists in identifying possible intertextual references. On the other hand, however, the variety of formulas requires careful inspection of the text in order to discern properly whether a text is cited. Further, introductory formulas do not always guarantee the correct identification of the referent text, and sometimes a reference to the OT will occur with no introductory formula or explicit marker. What becomes apparent here is the necessity of having clearly defined terms for the types of references found in the NT. While citations are usually accompanied by an introductory formula or marker, allusions and echoes are rarely accompanied by such clearly defined markers. Nonetheless, a better understanding of the citation techniques within this encyclopedia will assist in recognizing the intertextual references to Isaiah in 1 Peter.

Summary

The above aspects of a first-century Christian encyclopedia are by no means exhaustive, but are a sampling of the issues pertinent to the intertextual analysis of the Isaianic signs in 1 Peter. A knowledge of the historical and cultural context, textual tradition, and citation practices within the realm

---

30. See Ellis, *The Old Testament*, 82–87.

of encyclopedic knowledge will assist both in recognizing the intertextual references and in determining the purpose for their incorporation into the epistle. In the following analysis of the quotations, allusions, and echoes, new insights will be discovered about the encyclopedia in force during the composition of 1 Peter. In other words, the use of intertextual references to OT Scripture is just one entry found in the encyclopedia of 1 Peter.

5

"Signs" of Hope in 1 Peter

WITH THE UNIVERSE OF discourse of 1 Peter in place and the encyclopedia opened, the references to Isaiah in the epistle can be examined. In this intertextual step of the method, encyclopedic information surrounding the composition of 1 Peter is incorporated into the analysis. The encyclopedia and universe of discourse are brought together to determine how and why the intertextual references are employed; the two pillars of semiotic textual theory are not mutually exclusive.[1] The majority of this chapter will examine each Isaianic reference in 1 Peter through the lens of Peirce's sign triad in order to determine the function of the intertextual reference.

In chapter 2, Peirce's triadic sign model (sign, object, and interpretant) was presented as the operational model for examining the textual signs in this study. At this point, a description is provided of how these three elements of Peirce's sign triad relate to the Isaianic references in the epistle. First, a sign—something that stands for something to someone—is any reference to Isaiah *as it appears in 1 Peter*. According to a semiotic theory of textuality, a text is described as a verbal sign complex. In 1 Peter, the author incorporates references to Isaiah as signs; thus, the sign is not the original text of Isaiah, but the reference to Isaiah that is incorporated into 1 Peter.

---

1. Alkier makes this point precisely: "A 'universe of discourse' and an 'encyclopedia' thus stand in a hermeneutically reciprocal relationship. Only on the basis of the research of individual universes of discourse can reasonable entries be made into a virtual encyclopedia, but only through recourse to a postulated encyclopedia are manifested expressions actualized as content. It is a variation of the hermeneutical circle" ("New Testament Studies," 237).

Second, the object—that for which the sign stands—has two facets that need to be correlated. Since a sign is capable of representing an object in only one respect, it is impossible for a sign to stand for every facet of its object. Thus, Peirce distinguished between the immediate object and the dynamic object. The immediate object is the particular aspect of the object that is chosen to communicate its qualities, while the dynamic object is the object that motivates the generation of a sign and of which the immediate object represents only some particular aspect. Therefore, in accordance with Peirce's and Alkier's distinction, the dynamic object is the book of Isaiah and all its motifs and meanings located therein. The immediate object is the particular portion of the book of Isaiah from which the sign comes.

Finally, the third element of the sign triad is the intepretant. The interpretant is the further idea or sign created by the interactions between the sign (text of Isaiah in 1 Peter) and object (portion of Isaiah represented by the sign). A fundamental assumption of this study is that Isaiah is a major source for the author of 1 Peter. The latter was motivated by aspects of the book of Isaiah and incorporated textual signs into the composition of his epistle. Since the goal of this chapter is to determine the function of each Isaianic reference, this element of the triad will be examined in detail in the sections below. In summary of this first preliminary issue, each Isaianic reference in 1 Peter is a textual sign that points to an object (the book of Isaiah) and as a result produces an interpretant.

A semiotic method for studying texts does not stipulate a set of definitions or categories for intertextual references. As a result, the means for identifying and classifying the intertextual references must be either developed or adopted from other studies. Three terms will be employed in this study for identifying and classifying the references to Isaiah: quotation, allusion, and echo. One can view these terms along a spectrum moving from explicit to implicit. A quotation (used interchangeably with citation) is an explicit reference to another text that can be identified by either an introductory formula (e.g., καθὼς γέγραπται) or verbatim (or near verbatim) linguistic reproduction. An allusion is a less precise, implicit reference to a text that contains at least some linguistic commonalities with the source text. An echo is a vague, distant reference to a text, event, or story by the use of similar concepts or thoughts, which may or may not have any linguistic commonalities with the referent text.[2] The definitions of quotation, allu-

---

2. The distinction between allusion and echo is not a universal position. Some use one or the other, while others simply combine the two (i.e., allusive echo).

"Signs" of Hope in 1 Peter

sion, and echo will serve as the criteria for determining which texts in 1 Peter are from the book of Isaiah.

In the examination of the quotations, allusions, and echoes below, a table will be presented within the discussion of each intertextual reference that compares the Greek text of 1 Peter with the Greek text of Isaiah (OG). The tables will serve as the basis for the intertextual discussions. The analysis of each intertextual reference will proceed by identifying the Isaianic sign in 1 Peter, describing its object, and then determining its interpretant. The chapter will conclude with a summary statement of the results of the examination with a view to describing more completely the encyclopedia of Petrine Christianity. Conclusions also will be drawn regarding the application of a semiotic method to the intertextual references. By way of delimitation, this sort of intertextual study falls within the realm of Alkier's *limited* intertextuality and will focus only on the production-oriented approach to the references. A production-oriented perspective inquires as to which texts are cited, how this citation takes place, and the effects of meaning that result.

Quotations

For the present study a *quotation* (or *citation*) is defined as an explicit reference to another text that can be identified by either an introductory formula (e.g., καθὼς γέγραπται) and/or verbatim (or near verbatim) linguistic reproduction. The inclusion of the parenthetical *near verbatim* stems from the discussion of the textual tradition above. Occasionally, minor differences will exist between the Greek text of the NT and the LXX/OG due to the multiplicity of versions that were circulating in the first century. Defining a quotation as having near verbatim linguistic reproduction recognizes this difficulty and allows for slight deviation or difference. Only those texts that fall into the parameters of the definition of *quotation* have been chosen for analysis in this section.

The individual analyses of the intertextual references will proceed as follows. The sign will be identified in 1 Peter with a brief discussion on its form in the Greek text, noting any introductory formulas or explicit markers. Following this identification is a comparison of the text of the sign and the immediate object with a view to determining the textual tradition followed by the author. Then, the immediate object will be described further.[3] Here a concise statement of the context and setting of the object will

---

3. At the outset of this chapter, the dynamic object for this study was identified as

Defending Hope

be provided as a point of reference for the discussion of the interpretant. The pragmatic analysis in the previous chapter revealed that the story of the audience is presented as part of the larger story of salvation history. The Isaianic texts functioning as the immediate object are particular facets of this larger story; thus, in order to understand properly the immediate object, it is imperative to place oneself into 1 Peter's narrative universe by examining these portions of God's actions in history. Finally, the encyclopedic information will be accessed to assist in determining the interpretant of the sign-object relation.

One final note concerns the comparison of the quotations examined in this study with those listed in the UBS4 index. Of the seven texts deemed quotations in this section, UBS4 categorizes the last two, 1 Pet 3:14–15 and 4:14, as allusions. Also, on occasion, an additional verse or two may be provided in the tables for greater context. The Hebrew text has not been supplied in the tables, but a discussion of the Hebrew will be included in the individual analyses where pertinent.

Isaiah 40:6–8 in 1 Peter 1:24–25

The first Isaianic citation is located at the end of 1 Peter 1. The intertextual connection is illustrated below in table 4:

Table 4. Isaiah 40:6–8 in 1 Peter 1:24–25

1 Peter 1:24–25	Isaiah 40:6–8 (OG)
24 διότι πᾶσα σὰρξ ὡς χόρτος καὶ πᾶσα δόξα αὐτῆς ὡς ἄνθος χόρτου· ἐξηράνθη ὁ χόρτος καὶ τὸ ἄνθος ἐξέπεσεν· 25 τὸ δὲ ῥῆμα κυρίου μένει εἰς τὸν αἰῶνα. τοῦτο δέ ἐστιν τὸ ῥῆμα τὸ εὐαγγελισθὲν εἰς ὑμᾶς.	6 φωνὴ λέγοντος βόησον καὶ εἶπα τί βοήσω πᾶσα σὰρξ χόρτος καὶ πᾶσα δόξα ἀνθρώπου ὡς ἄνθος χόρτου 7 ἐξηράνθη ὁ χόρτος καὶ τὸ ἄνθος ἐξέπεσεν 8 τὸ δὲ ῥῆμα τοῦ θεοῦ ἡμῶν μένει εἰς τὸν αἰῶνα

Recognition of this of this text is aided by the use of the explicit marker διότι in 1:24 preceding the citation. Moreover, immediately followig the citation in v. 25 is a second marker resembling the *pesher*-like formula τοῦτο ἐστιν. Together these two markers bracket the citation. The immediate object is

---

the entire book of Isaiah. Since each Isaianic sign in 1 Peter presents only one aspect of this dynamic object, a discussion on the latter will be deferred until the summary section of this chapter after each immediate object has been studied.

identified as Isa 40:6–8, some differences exist between the text of 1 Peter and the texts of the OG and MT.

Initially, it seems the author relied on the OG when quoting this text.[4] Following are three major differences among the texts. First, the author inserted ὡς between σάρξ and χόρτος, thus turning the metaphor into a simile; but this difference can be explained by the author's stylistic penchant for ὡς, as it occurs in many other places in the epistle. Second, the author used the genitive form of λόγος in v. 23 to describe "the living and enduring word of God," but in v. 25 (after the quotation) he used the word ῥῆμα to describe the word that was preached to them. The use of ῥῆμα in v. 25b most likely is due to its presence in the quotation in v. 25a, which is the same reading found in the OG. In addition, both words refer to the same concept of reality, so no major problem is presented with this difference in wording.[5]

The third, and most significant, difference between the OT text and the quotation in 1 Peter is the replacement of τοῦ θεοῦ (the reading in both OG and MT) with κυρίου. This change could be the result of the author's use of a variant OG text, a quotation from memory, or a deliberate theological change of the text. Elliott adamantly argues the latter point, concluding that this understanding coheres with the author's statement about prophetic action in 1:11–12, which indicates the prophets spoke about Christ. The latter view takes κυρίου as an objective genitive, that is, "the word about the Lord."[6] In other words, in this context Jesus is the content of the ῥῆμα.

Isaiah 40:6–8 (the immediate object) is a passage situated in a contrast between unfaithful Israel and the faithful God.[7] Isaiah 40:1 begins with

---

4. Moyise and Menken, *Isaiah*, 176, outlined the four major differences between the Masoretic Text (MT) and LXX (they use this designation instead of OG) texts and showed how the author of 1 Peter agrees with the MT on one point but sides with the LXX on the other three.

5. Achtemeier, *1 Peter*, 142, remarked, "It is the living and abiding word (λόγος) of God, by which they have been rebegotten, which is at work in the proclamation (ῥῆμα) of the gospel."

6. So Elliott, *1 Peter*, 391; Michaels, *1 Peter*, 79.

7. The author is aware of the various understandings of the authorship and setting of the book of Isaiah. For the sake of brevity, the following comments provide the stance taken on authorship, setting, and the message of Isaiah in this study. The author is the prophet Isaiah who, through predictive prophecy, addresses a variety of historical settings of the eighth, seventh, and sixth centuries B.C. The drastic political times during these centuries have a direct effect on the religious atmosphere of the people of God as they seek answers to the unfolding events of history. Primary themes that emerge from Isaiah are servanthood, trust, hope, and restoration. Seminal and more recent works that address these issues in greater detail include Duhm, *Das Buch Jesaia*; Torrey, *The Second*

Defending Hope

a comforting word to a people who are in distress and disarray due to the Babylonian exile. In the midst of this exilic judgment for their sin, the Lord provides the context for his faithfulness. The people of Israel are compared to grass and their glory to the flower of the field, both of which pass away in due time. On the other hand, the word of the Lord endures forever. In effect, Isaiah communicates the physical weakness and unreliability of the flesh while demonstrating the lasting nature of the word of the Lord, and this word holds the promise of future restoration for God's chosen people.

Prior to this quotation in 1 Peter, the author states that his addressees have been born again of imperishable seed through the living and enduring word of God (1:23). The quotation from Isaiah 40 is not merely a proof-text for v. 23, but a confirmation of the contrast between mankind and God illustrated in Isaiah. In 1 Peter, the people represent the perishable seed and the word of God represents the imperishable seed. The enduring nature of God's word provides the motivation for patience and endurance in the difficult situation surrounding the audience of 1 Peter. Thus, the interpretant for this sign is a message of hope reinforced by the enduring nature of God's word. The ῥῆμα spoken to the readers of Isaiah (which was the promise of restoration from exile) is similar to the message or ῥῆμα of the gospel as it pertains to the historical setting of the audience of 1 Peter.

Isaianic Quotations in 1 Peter 2:6–9

A concentration of three Isaianic citations is found in 1 Pet 2:6–9. The first two (from Isa 28:16 and 8:14) are cited frequently in the NT to identify Jesus as the cornerstone and commonly are referred to as the *stone* citations.[8] The third (from Isa 43:20–21) comments on the identity of the people of God, and, contrasted with the stone citations, is sometimes referred to as one of the *people* citations. Due to this high concentration of Isaianic texts in such a short section of 1 Peter, the three references will be examined together under this one section. Before examining each intertextual reference, the author first will summarize the literary context of 1 Peter in which the citations are situated.

Isaiah; Westermann, *Isaiah 40-66*; Achtemeier, *Community and Message*; Watts, *Isaiah 1-33*; Oswalt, *Isaiah 1-39*; Watts, *Isaiah 34-66*; Sweeney, *Isaiah 1-39*; Oswalt, *Isaiah 40-66*; Baltzer, *Deutero-Isaiah*; and Childs, *Isaiah*.

8. The locations of these texts in the NT are Mark 12:10-11; Matt 21:42-44; Luke 20:17-18; Acts 4:11-12; Rom 9:32-33; Eph 2:20-22; and 1 Pet 2:4-8.

"Signs" of Hope in 1 Peter

Each of the three quotations is part of the larger section of 2:4–10, which is a combination of both stone and people citations from the OT.[9] The only three stone texts in the OT are found in Ps 118:22–23, Isa 8:14–15, and Isa 28:16. A unique feature of 1 Pet 2:4–10 is that nowhere else in the NT are these three stone texts placed together.[10] Verses 4 and 5 function as an introduction to the cited texts in vv. 6–8 with the use of phrases such as "living stones" (v. 4) and "a holy priesthood" (v. 5).[11] Closing out this pericope are citations and allusions to the people of God in vv. 9–10. Therefore, 1 Pet 2:4–10 closes the first major section of the epistle's body (1:13—2:10) with a forceful reminder to his readers about their new identity in Christ. The author combines elements of the stone tradition and people passages in a unique way to describe both Christ and the Christian community.

The first citation examined is that of Isa 28:16 in 1 Pet 2:6, as table 5 below illustrates:

Table 5. Isaiah 28:16 in 1 Peter 2:6

1 Peter 2:6	Isaiah 28:16 (OG)
διότι περιέχει ἐν γραφῇ· ἰδοὺ τίθημι ἐν Σιὼν λίθον ἀκρογωνιαῖον ἐκλεκτὸν ἔντιμον καὶ ὁ πιστεύων ἐπ' αὐτῷ οὐ μὴ καταισχυνθῇ.	διὰ τοῦτο οὕτως λέγει κύριος ἰδοὺ ἐγὼ ἐμβαλῶ εἰς τὰ θεμέλια Σιων λίθον πολυτελῆ ἐκλεκτὸν ἀκρογωνιαῖον ἔντιμον εἰς τὰ θεμέλια αὐτῆς καὶ ὁ πιστεύων ἐπ' αὐτῷ οὐ μὴ καταισχυνθῇ

A recognizable introductory formula (διότι περιέχει ἐν γραφῇ, "for it stands/says in Scripture") signals the citation. The OG translation of Isa 28:16, the immediate object, exhibits one significant difference from the MT that also appears in Peter's citation of this text. In the MT, the final clause of the verse states, "The one who trusts will not hasten" (figuratively,

---

9. Five notable articles on these passages are Snodgrass, "1 Peter 2:1–10," 97–106; Oss, "Interpretation," 181–200; van Rensburg and Moyise, "1 Peter 2:4–10," 12–30; Williams, "A Case Study," 37–55; and Koch, "The Quotations," 223–40.

10. In Rom 9:33, Paul conflates both Isa 28:16 and 8:14, but he does not include the stone text of Psalm 118. On this point, Jobes and Silva suggest that Paul and Peter might be reflecting an early Christian tradition in linking these two Isaianic texts. Due to the dependence of both apostles, in large part, on the OG text for the same citations, Jobes and Silva rightly conclude that "the Greek translator's own reflection on the message of Isaiah had a significant impact on early Christian theology" (*Invitation to the Septuagint*, 199).

11. As a sort of introduction, these phrases have more of an allusive function in the text. Therefore, this aspect is examined in the section on allusions below.

"to hasten" would mean "to panic" or "to be dismayed"). Both the OG and NT insert in this clause the prepositional phrase ἐπ' αὐτῷ. This phrase can be translated one of two ways. If the antecedent is λίθον, then the translation would be "in it." If the phrase is taken to refer to the messiah, then the translation would be "in him."[12] Nonetheless, Peter shows dependence on the OG in citing this Isaianic text.

The context of the immediate object is a call to Israel to seek security in God instead of the surrounding nations. Isaiah 28 begins with a woe to Ephraim for disobeying the Lord. Isaiah condemns the sin of the priests and prophets, both of whom are drunk with wine. He then predicts their captivity and exile would be carried out by another nation. In vv. 14–15, he rebukes the leaders of Jerusalem for making "a covenant with death" and "a pact with Sheol," probably referring to a military or political pact Israel had made with a foreign nation for the purpose of security. In reality, this covenant provided only a false sense of security. Thus, in v. 16 the Lord states that he is laying a "chosen and precious cornerstone" and "he who believes will not be dismayed." In contrast to the unstable security offered by allied nations of Israel, the only true source of security and salvation is presented as a refuge with a sure foundation. In effect, Israel is directed to move away from this false sense of security toward their only hope of security and prosperity; it is a call to return to faith and trust in Yahweh.

The OT texts presented in 2:6–7 unpack what was introduced in 2:4; namely, that Christ is the chosen and precious cornerstone who was rejected by mankind but in whom the audience finds honor (οὐ μὴ καταισχυνθῇ).[13] Comfort is offered through this citation because just as Christ was rejected by mankind despite being chosen by God, so also the audience of 1 Peter will experience rejection and suffering though they are God's elect (1:1; 2:9). While this citation certainly would create an image of hope, perhaps the interpretant is made more explicit in the verse immediately following the citation. Isaiah 28:17 (OG) begins καὶ θήσω κρίσιν εἰς ἐλπίδα ("I will turn judgment into hope").[14] If the believing audience is being built into a

---

12. Jobes, *1 Peter*, 147, cites evidence from *Tg. Ps.-J.* and 1QS 8:8 that might argue for a messianic interpretation of Isa 28:16 that predates the Christological use of this text in the NT.

13. In addition, Moyise and Menken, *Isaiah*, 180, noted that ἔντιμον (precious) is a cognate of τιμή (honor, 2:7).

14. The OG reading differs from the MT, which reads, "I will make justice the measuring line."

"Signs" of Hope in 1 Peter

metaphorical "spiritual house" (2:5), then their hope is rooted in Christ as the cornerstone of this building.

The second citation in this short section is found in 1 Pet 2:8, as table 6 illustrates below:

Table 6. Isaiah 8:14 in 1 Peter 2:8

1 Peter 2:8	Isaiah 8:14 (OG)
καὶ λίθος προσκόμματος καὶ πέτρα σκανδάλου· οἳ προσκόπτουσιν τῷ λόγῳ ἀπειθοῦντες εἰς ὃ καὶ ἐτέθησαν.	καὶ ἐὰν ἐπ' αὐτῷ πεποιθὼς ᾖς ἔσται σοι εἰς ἁγίασμα καὶ οὐχ ὡς λίθου προσκόμματι συναντήσεσθε αὐτῷ οὐδὲ ὡς πέτρας πτώματι ὁ δὲ οἶκος Ιακωβ ἐν παγίδι καὶ ἐν κοιλάσματι ἐγκαθήμενοι ἐν Ιερουσαλημ

While no introductory formula is used to introduce the citation, the καὶ preceding the text could be identified as an explicit marker. Here, the καὶ conjoins the Isaianic citation in v. 8 with the previous citation of Ps 118:22 in v. 7. The immediate object is identified as Isa 8:14. The linguistic similarities between the NT and OG are apparent, but upon closer examination it appears Peter follows the MT over against the OG. First, in the OG, λίθου and πέτρας are genitive due to their comparative use with ὡς. In 1 Pet 2:8, the comparative ὡς is taken out and the two nouns are changed to nominatives; thus, what is a simile in the OG is transformed into a factual statement by Peter. Second, Peter's use of σκανδάλου ("that which causes stumbling") instead of πτώματι ("that which has fallen") is a more accurate rendering of the Hebrew *mikšôl*.

The setting of the immediate object, Isaiah 8, has as its historical backdrop a setting of political tension. Ahaz sends a plea for help to the Assyrian king Tiglath-pileser against the Syro-Ephraimite coalition of Pekah and Rezin. This desperate plea so displeased the Lord that he instructed Isaiah not to follow the way of the people in this matter. Therefore, the warning uttered by God in Isa 8:11–15 is not directed toward the people in general, but Isaiah and his disciples in particular. Isaiah is not to fear what the people fear (the military forces of surrounding nations), but he is to fear and revere God alone. Isaiah 8:14, the text quoted in 1 Peter, states how God will become a stumbling stone and a snare for the Israelites since they place their trust and hope in allies rather than in God. At the same time, however, he will be a sanctuary for Isaiah and everyone who places their trust in him.

Defending Hope

First Peter 2:7–8 provides the negative counterpart to v. 6. In 2:6, Peter reiterates honor and hope in Christ as the cornerstone for those who believe. Verses 7–8 speak of the effect of the cornerstone on unbelievers; that is, they stumble over it and are brought to shame.[15] Thus, the interpretant for this citation resembles that of the previous one. Hope comes through the effects of the cornerstone on those who disbelieve—who, in this case, may be the ones responsible for the suffering of the audience.

The third, and final, Isaianic sign in this section comes in 1 Pet 2:9. Table 7 illustrates the intertextual connection as follows:

Table 7. Isaiah 43:20–21 in 1 Peter 2:9

1 Peter 2:9	Isaiah 43:20–21 (OG)
ὑμεῖς δὲ γένος ἐκλεκτόν, βασίλειον ἱεράτευμα, ἔθνος ἅγιον, λαὸς εἰς περιποίησιν, ὅπως τὰς ἀρετὰς ἐξαγγείλητε τοῦ ἐκ σκότους ὑμᾶς καλέσαντος εἰς τὸ θαυμαστὸν αὐτοῦ φῶς	20 εὐλογήσει με τὰ θηρία τοῦ ἀγροῦ σειρῆνες καὶ θυγατέρες στρουθῶν ὅτι ἔδωκα ἐν τῇ ἐρήμῳ ὕδωρ καὶ ποταμοὺς ἐν τῇ ἀνύδρῳ ποτίσαι τὸ γένος μου τὸ ἐκλεκτόν 21 λαόν μου ὃν περιεποιησάμην τὰς ἀρετάς μου διηγεῖσθαι

No introductory formula or explicit marker is found in this verse. The way in which the author previously strung together various citations in vv. 6–8, combined with his penchant for concluding a major section with a citation, increases the likelihood of a reference to Scripture in the final two verses of the first section of the epistle's body. In vv. 6–8, Peter employs Scripture to describe Christ (v. 5) and how his identity as the cornerstone affects both believers and nonbelievers. Now, in vv. 9–10, the discussion shifts to the identity of the audience. Thus, even though the particle de; does not usually function as a formula or marker, in this literary context it seems to be used as such.

For 1 Pet 2:9, two immediate objects actually can be identified: Isa 43:20–21 and Exod 19:6. The verse in Peter contains four phrases commenting on the audience's identity and one final clause indicating their purpose. Only the first and fourth statements on identity ("a chosen people/race" and "a people for possession") and the purpose statement ("in order

---

15. Michaels, *1 Peter*, 106–7, addresses the connection between stumbling (v. 8) and shame (v. 6), noting that "if there is a difference between 'stumbling' and 'shame,' it is that the latter is more future-oriented and final (cf. 3:16), while the former describes for Peter the present state of the disobedient (note the present verb προσκόπτουσιν)."

that you might proclaim the praises") are from Isa 43:20–21; the second and third identity statements ("a royal priesthood" and "a holy nation") are from Exod 19:6. Concerning the Isaianic objects, the phrase γένος ἐκλεκτόν occurs only in Isa 43:20 (OG) in the OT.[16] Isaiah 43:21 further describes this chosen people as "the people I acquired (περιεποιησάμην) for myself to recount (διηγεῖσθαι) my praises (τὰς ἀρετάς)." Three differences between the reading in 1 Peter and that in the OG can be noted.

First, the verbal form περιεποιησάμην is changed to a nominal form in 1 Peter (περιποίησιν). Second, in Isaiah the verb διηγεῖσθαι means "to recount," whereas in 1 Peter the verb ἐξαγγείλητε means "to proclaim."[17] Finally, whereas in the OG the infinitive is used with the noun τὰς ἀρετάς, in 1 Peter this construction is altered to a purpose clause with the preparatory use of ὅπως. Since the OG forms of these words agree with the reading in the MT, the most likely conclusion is that the author followed the Greek reading for this citation.

In situating the immediate object, Isaiah 43 is essentially an exhortation both to be comforted and to trust in God's comfort. The first seven verses of this chapter exhort the people not to fear but to hope in God. Verses 8–13 communicate the sovereignty of God and the people as witnesses of his sovereignty. Then, vv. 14–21, the section in which the quotation in 1 Peter occurs, are a call not to reflect on the former things God has done for the people (i.e., deliverance from Egypt and safe passage through the Red Sea), but to watch for something new that God will do (43:19). The "new (thing)" could be a reference to their deliverance out of Babylonian captivity. Like the first exodus, God will once again deliver his people from exile (thus resembling a sort of second exodus). Despite this good news, Isaiah 43 ends with a word of judgment to the people because of their transgression and disobedience. Nevertheless, in this text God outlines who his people are to be and what they are to do (43:10, 21).

The interpretant of this sign-object relation could evoke images of hope and judgment. In light of the situation of the audience, Peter's use of Scripture to remind them of their identity is hopeful on account of both

---

16. The only other place this exact wording is found is in the apocryphal Add Esth 16:21 (8:12) in the LXX.

17. This change is the most surprising especially since ἐξαγγέλω is used nowhere else in the NT (except in the textually questionable shorter ending of Mark). Michaels's suggestion (1 Peter, 110) that the OT referent also might be Ps 9:15 deserves further consideration. This text not only uses ἐξαγγέλω but also has the construction ὅπως + the subjunctive (which is the exact construction in 1 Pet 2:9).

Defending Hope

their election (1:1; 2:9) and the deliverance God can provide (Isa 43:19). Yet, this same reminder goes well with the statements made by Peter in the previous verses on what the outcome is for those who do not believe (i.e., they stumble). The audience must cling to their belief and hope in God or the outcome will not be so favorable (cf. Isa 43:28).

Isaiah 53:9 in 1 Peter 2:22

In 1 Pet 2:18–25, the author provides an exhortation for slaves to be obedient to their masters, whether the latter are good or evil. Accompanying this exhortation is the example *par excellence* of obedience in suffering: Jesus Christ. In the final four verses of this section (2:22–25), Peter supplies a cluster of six references to Isaiah 53, traditionally designated as one of the Servant Songs of Isaiah.[18] Of these references, only the first, Isa 53:9 in 1 Pet 2:22, can be viewed as a quotation with the other references serving as allusions (discussed in the next subsection). Table 8 shows the intertextual relationship of this Isaianic sign and its immediate object.

Table 8. Isaiah 53:9 in 1 Peter 2:22

1 Peter 2:21–22	Isaiah 53:9 (OG)
21 εἰς τοῦτο γὰρ ἐκλήθητε, ὅτι καὶ Χριστὸς ἔπαθεν ὑπὲρ ὑμῶν ὑμῖν ὑπολιμπάνων ὑπογραμμὸν ἵνα ἐπακολουθήσητε τοῖς ἴχνεσιν αὐτοῦ, 22 ὃς ἁμαρτίαν οὐκ ἐποίησεν οὐδὲ εὑρέθη δόλος ἐν τῷ στόματι αὐτοῦ	καὶ δώσω τοὺς πονηροὺς ἀντὶ τῆς ταφῆς αὐτοῦ καὶ τοὺς πλουσίους ἀντὶ τοῦ θανάτου αὐτοῦ ὅτι ἀνομίαν οὐκ ἐποίησεν οὐδὲ εὑρέθη δόλος ἐν τῷ στόματι αὐτοῦ

Due to the lack of an introductory marker or formula, the connection between this sign and the immediate object (Isa 53:9) relies on linguistic correspondence alone. As table 8 demonstrates, the citation matches almost exactly the text of the OG. The two differences are Peter's replacement of

---

18. The four Servant Songs are Isaiah 42, 49, 50, and 52–53. In the early church, the fourth Servant Song was used extensively to refer to the suffering of Jesus. As Davids commented, "It is so interwoven that the writer flows unconsciously from citation of Isaiah into description of the crucifixion, for he is using formulas long established in the church" (*First Epistle of Peter*, 110). Davids further proposed that "the whole section from 2:22 to 2:25 has a rhythmic character that makes it likely that Peter is using an already known creedal formula of the church" (110, n. 17).

ἀνομίαν ("lawlessness") with ἁμαρτίαν ("sin") and the inclusion of the relative pronoun ὅς, which connects this text to Christ (v. 21).

All four Servant Songs hold in common a variety of themes intended to encourage a post-exilic community. Since the exodus is viewed as the great paradigm for the salvation and deliverance of Israel, the fact that the Servant Songs exhibit exodus typology connecting their Babylonian captivity to their former bondage in Egypt is not surprising. The purpose of the servant passages is to communicate the physical and spiritual salvation ushered in by the servant. Isaiah 53 highlights specific characteristics of God's holy servant and events accompanying this servant. The passage speaks of the servant being lifted up and exalted, despised and rejected by mankind, stricken and afflicted by God, and wounded and chastised for the benefit of the people. Thus, the immediate object is located in a context of encouragement and hope.

As a paradigm for handling suffering, the citation in 1 Pet 2:22 brings about an interpretant of hope. Hope is communicated through this citation precisely by confirming that there is an example (ὑπογραμμὸν) to follow (v. 21). Peter's reference to Isaiah 53 portrays Christ as the Suffering Servant who is to be emulated by the suffering slaves whom the author addresses.[19] Moreover, an additional effect of the quotation was to draw the reader to the larger context of the entire Servant Song, thus preparing the reader for the multiple allusions that follow in vv. 23–25.[20] By way of contrast, this conclusion is exactly the opposite of the one reached concerning Peter's use of Isaiah in 1 Pet 2. In 2:4–5, he first alludes to Isaianic texts, and these allusions prepare the way for the citations that follow in 2:6–9. Already at this point in the investigation it is clear Peter does not follow a rigid format for referencing texts, as is evidenced in both his sequencing of allusions and citations and his varying use of introductory formulas or explicit markers.

Isaiah 8:12–13 in 1 Peter 3:14–15

A reference to Isa 8:12–13 occurs at the beginning of the third body section (3:13—4:11).

---

19. Moyise and Menken, *Isaiah*, 183–84, concluded that Peter's reworking of the Isaiah 53 material communicates Jesus's innocence and non-retaliation, Jesus's accomplishment, and the reader's predicament and salvation.

20. For a helpful chart detailing the correspondences between Isaiah 53 and 1 Pet 2:21–25, see Elliott, *1 Peter*, 547.

Defending Hope

Table 9. Isaiah 8:12-13 in 1 Peter 3:14-15

1 Peter 3:14-15	Isaiah 8:12-13 (OG)
14 ἀλλ᾽ εἰ καὶ πάσχοιτε διὰ δικαιοσύνην, μακάριοι. Τὸν δὲ φόβον αὐτῶν μὴ φοβηθῆτε μηδὲ ταραχθῆτε, 15 κύριον δὲ τὸν Χριστὸν ἁγιάσατε ἐν ταῖς καρδίαις ὑμῶν, ἕτοιμοι ἀεί πρὸς ἀπολογίαν παντὶ τῷ αἰτοῦντι ὑμᾶς λόγον περὶ τῆς ἐν ὑμῖν ἐλπίδος	12 μήποτε εἴπητε σκληρόν πᾶν γάρ ὃ ἐὰν εἴπῃ ὁ λαὸς οὗτος σκληρόν ἐστιν τὸν δὲ φόβον αὐτοῦ οὐ μὴ φοβηθῆτε οὐδὲ μὴ ταραχθῆτε 13 κύριον αὐτὸν ἁγιάσατε καὶ αὐτὸς ἔσται σου φόβος

Like the previous citation, no introductory markers are present to signal this citation in the text. Several items, though, would point to this text as a citation.[21] First, the insertion of the unusual phrase τὸν δὲ φόβον—occurring only in Isa 8:12 and Prov 1:29 in the OG—is abrupt in the text of 1 Peter. Second, 1 Peter continues with the order of the text of Isaiah by including the verbs φοβηθῆτε and ταραχθῆτε (same form as in the OG). Third, 1 Pet 3:15 provides the command to sanctify (ἁγιάσατε) the Lord, as is stated in Isa 8:13. Finally, the author's citation of Isa 8:14 in 2:8 lends credence to this being a citation as well. The situation is similar to that in 2:4-10. In the latter, Peter alludes to concepts in vv. 4-5 that he expounds upon through citations in vv. 6-9. By virtue of the citation of Isa 8 in 1 Pet 2:8, the context of Isa 8 already has been evoked within the narrative world. Thus, another reference to Isa 8 would not have been unexpected. Moreover, the use of δὲ in 3:14, though part of the OG text, might mirror its use as an explicit marker in 2:9. Based on the aforementioned reasons, the sign in 1 Pet 3:14-15 has Isa 8:12-13 as its immediate object.

As was stated in the discussion of 1 Pet 2:8, the situation of Isa 8 is the Lord's displeasure with Israel's dependence on political alliances over against the provision and protection that only he can provide. As a result, God speaks directly to Isaiah and tells him not to follow the people in their dealings and, in this case, not to fear what they fear (8:12) but to set God apart as Lord (8:13). In Isaiah, the genitive αὐτοῦ is taken as subjective: "Do not fear what they fear." In 1 Peter, however, if the genitive αὐτῶν refers to the opponents in the previous verse who cause their suffering, then understanding this as a subjective genitive would be irrelevant for the audience. An objective genitive ("Do not fear *them*") is more likely the nuance

---

21. For a concise discussion of the issues pertaining to this citation, see Moyise and Menken, *Isaiah*, 184-85; and van Rensburg and Moyise, "1 Peter 3:13-17," 275-86.

considering the context.²² The contrast is brought out explicitly in both the MT and OG in Isa 8:13b: "He will be your fear and he will be your dread" (MT) and simply "He will be your fear" (OG). Though this portion of Isa 8:13 is not cited in 1 Peter, the contrast is still perceivable in the exhortation to them to sanctify Christ alone.²³

Whereas the purpose for quoting from Isaiah 8 in 1 Pet 2:8 was to portray Christ as the cornerstone, the purpose for quoting from the same Isaianic context here in 1 Pet 3 is to encourage the readers as they suffer for righteousness' sake (3:14a). Further, the second part of the citation indicates that believers should sanctify Christ alone when in the face of danger or persecution.²⁴ In other words, this suffering people is to be unafraid before mankind, but fearful before God. The interpretant for this sign-object relation could be described as boldness in the face of suffering. As a caveat, an intriguing point here is how Peter has utilized the same immediate object (Isaiah 8) to communicate two different concepts about the dynamic object (book of Isaiah).²⁵

Isaiah 11:2 in 1 Peter 4:14

In 1 Pet 4:12–19, the author places Christian suffering in an eschatological context with implications for both present and future living. He instructs his audience to rejoice in the midst of suffering and to consider themselves blessed when they are reviled for the name of Christ. The latter point is followed in 4:14b with the clause "for the spirit of glory and of God rests on you." In table 10 below, this text is identified as the sign which stands for Isa 11:2, its immediate object.

---

22. See Moyise and Menken, *Isaiah*, 185. Selwyn, *St. Peter*, 192, relates it as follows: "But φόβος can take either a subjective genitive (fear felt *by* someone) or an objective genitive (fear felt *of* someone); and, even if the former was the construction in Is. viii. 12, St. Peter was fully entitled to use the latter construction here."

23. Surprisingly, van Rensburg and Moyise, "1 Peter 3:13–17," 283–85, disregard Isa 8:13b in favor of a third text (Isa 51:12–13), which they believe functions as an echo and explains the meaning of the citation.

24. Peter's replacement of αὐτὸν (Isa 8:13 OG, the antecedent is God) with Χριστὸν (1 Pet 3:15) seemingly introduces a tension into the text. On the contrary, it is unlikely that he is suggesting his audience should stop sanctifying God and start sanctifying Christ, since this change was common in Christian exegesis (e.g., Phil 2:10) and since Christological arguments are assumed in at least two other places (1:25; 2:3). For more on this citation, see van Rensburg and Moyise, "1 Peter 3:13–17," 282–83.

25. Cf. the discussion of this citation with that of Isa 8:14 in 1 Pet 2:8 above.

Defending Hope

Table 10. Isaiah 11:2 in 1 Peter 4:14

1 Peter 4:14	Isaiah 11:2 (OG)
εἰ ὀνειδίζεσθε ἐν ὀνόματι Χριστοῦ, μακάριοι, ὅτι τὸ τῆς δόξης καὶ τὸ τοῦ θεοῦ πνεῦμα ἐφ' ὑμᾶς ἀναπαύεται.	καὶ ἀναπαύσεται ἐπ' αὐτὸν πνεῦμα τοῦ θεοῦ πνεῦμα σοφίας καὶ συνέσεως πνεῦμα βουλῆς καὶ ἰσχύος πνεῦμα γνώσεως καὶ εὐσεβείας

While many Petrine scholars take this scriptural reference to be an allusion, the reference is classified here as a citation for the following two reasons: (1) the only place in the LXX where πνεῦμα, θεός, and ἀναπαύω occur together is in Isa 11:2; and (2) the reference is preceded by the explicit marker ὅτι.

Three major differences exist between the citation and the OG text. First, Peter adds the phrase τὸ τῆς δόξης to the citation, but this addition appears to function as a hendiadys with τὸ τοῦ θεοῦ. The first definite article in both constructions is connected to πνεῦμα; therefore, if taken as appositives, the resulting translation would be "the spirit of glory, the spirit of God."[26] Additionally, the insertion of this phrase is consistent with other references to "glory" in this section (cf. 4:11, 12, 13, 16). The second difference is the change of αὐτὸν ("him") to the plural ὑμᾶς ("you"). In effect, Peter shifts the promise of the spirit from the "shoot of Jesse" (Isa 11:1) to his audience. Finally, the third change is the shift of the future tense verb ἀναπαύσεται (OG) to the present tense ἀναπαύεται in 1 Peter. Based on this verbal substitution, it seems that Peter viewed the prophecy in Isaiah as having its fulfillment with the community of Christian readers to whom he is writing.

In the context of the immediate object, a messianic ruler ("a shoot from the stem of Jesse") is described. This ruler will lead and judge Israel in righteousness and faithfulness. In Isa 11:2, the text states that the spirit of the Lord will rest upon him along with the spirit of wisdom, understanding, counsel, might, knowledge, and fear of the Lord.[27] The reign of this ruler is described as a peaceful time when the earth is full of the knowledge of the Lord (vv. 6–10). That God's Spirit rests on him indicates he will be a successful ruler, one on whom God has placed his stamp of approval.

As Elliott noted, this is only one of a few references to the Spirit in the Epistle of 1 Peter, and here "reproach because of Christ is a sure sign

---

26. Elliott, *1 Peter*, 782, argued for this understanding as well, but rendered this pleonastic construction as "the divine Spirit of glory."

27. In fact, more than thirty times in the LXX the Spirit (πνεῦμα) of God is described as being upon (ἐπί) someone.

"Signs" of Hope in 1 Peter

of the Spirit's immediate presence."[28] Likewise, Feldmeier commented that "the promise of the presence of God's Spirit is contrasted with the oppressive present experience of suffering, which Spirit for its part is a 'pledge' of participation in the divine glory (2 Cor 1:22; cf. Rom 8:23)."[29] The quotation from the Isaiah passage communicates to the audience of 1 Peter that when they suffer not only are they blessed, but they can also be comforted because the very Spirit of God rests on them. Paul speaks of a similar concept when he states that the riches of the mystery of God is "Christ in you, the hope of glory" (Col 1:27). Therefore, the resulting interpretant is the evocation of comfort and hope.

Allusions and Echoes

Allusions and echoes are treated together in one section because, due to their commonalities, they are usually more difficult to distinguish. The source text for allusions and echoes is often debatable since the linguistic similarities might not be as noticeable as with quotations. Moreover, allusions and echoes are usually not accompanied by an introductory formula or explicit marker. For this subsection the definitions of both terms will determine which texts are chosen for analysis. An allusion is a less precise, implicit reference to a text that contains at least some linguistic commonalities with the source text. An echo is a vague, distant reference to a text, event, or story by the use of similar concepts or thoughts that may or may not have any linguistic commonalities with the referent text. The numerous texts examined in this section will demonstrate the depth of Peter's interaction with Isaiah.

Eight allusions and one echo are examined in this subsection. By way of comparison, the singular echo (Isa 48:10 in 1 Pet 1:7) is deemed an allusion in UBS4. Also, one of the allusions (Isa 52:3 in 1 Pet 1:18) in this study is not listed at all in the UBS4 index.[30] Due to the nature of allusions

---

28. Elliott, *1 Peter*, 783.

29. Feldmeier, *First Letter of Peter*, 226. Elliott, *1 Peter*, 782, notes that a connection between suffering and glory appears elsewhere in 1 Peter (1:11; 5:1, 10) and also in 2 Cor 4:17.

30. Three references that were not chosen for analysis, but deserve mention, are: Isa 61:6 in 1 Pet 2:9; Isa 42:12 in 1 Pet 2:9; and Isa 28:5 in 1 Pet 5:4. The first two references—both of which are deemed allusions by UBS4 and are found in 1 Pet 2:9—are not included because Isa 43:20–21 and Exod 19:6 provide the most explicit connections with the content of 1 Pet 2:9. Finally, Isa 28:5 and 1 Pet 5:4 share two linguistic similarities, but this reference does not meet the criteria of the definitions for allusion and echo.

Defending Hope

and echoes, the individual analyses will differ slightly from those in the previous section. In each of the texts below, no introductory formulas or explicit markers are present. Additionally, the discussion of the form of the allusion or echo will be abbreviated since the linguistic similarities might not be as explicit. Emphasis will be placed on the literary contexts of both the sign and the immediate object, and the proposed interpretant will be offered. The tables accompanying each reference follow the same formatting as those in the Quotations section above.

Isaiah 48:10 in 1 Peter 1:7

The very first intertextual reference in 1 Peter is an echo of Isa 48:10. The Isaianic sign is located in 1 Pet 1:7 in the introduction to the epistle, as table 11 illustrates below.

Table 11. Isaiah 48:10 in 1 Peter 1:7

1 Peter 1:7	Isaiah 48:10 (OG)
ἵνα τὸ δοκίμιον ὑμῶν τῆς πίστεως πολυτιμότερον χρυσίου τοῦ ἀπολλυμένου διὰ πυρὸς δὲ δοκιμαζομένου, εὑρεθῇ εἰς ἔπαινον καὶ δόξαν καὶ τιμὴν ἐν ἀποκαλύψει Ἰησοῦ Χριστοῦ:	ἰδοὺ πέπρακά σε οὐχ ἕνεκεν ἀργυρίου ἐξειλάμην δέ σε ἐκ καμίνου πτωχείας

For this sign-object relation, no linguistic similarities exist between the 1 Peter text and either the OG or MT.[31] Not even the precious metal mentioned is the same ("gold" in 1 Peter, "silver" in OG and MT). Despite the lack of verbal similarities, one primary conceptual connection appears with reference to the process of refining. The MT includes the verb meaning "to refine" (*sĕraptîkā*), while the Greek of 1 Peter describes this process pleonastically (with the use of δοκίμιον, χρυσίου, τοῦ ἀπολλυμένου διὰ πυρὸς, and εὑρεθῇ). In light of these comments, this reference is best deemed an echo.

The context of the immediate object, Isa 48:10, is God's refinement of disobedient Israel. The Lord shows great patience and mercy with his people

---

31. The OG reading is different from the MT. The former states, with the differences in italics, "Behold, I have *sold* you not for the sake of silver, but I have rescued you from the furnace of *poverty*."

"Signs" of Hope in 1 Peter

by declaring a delay of his wrath (48:9) and testing them only through affliction (48:10).[32] At the end of the chapter the Lord tells the people to go out from Babylon with shouts of joy, proclaiming that the Lord has delivered them from captivity. Interestingly, the following chapter, Isaiah 49, is one of the servant songs. In this chapter the servant is identified as Israel (v. 3), and his mission is to bring God's salvation to all the earth (v. 6). Elements of refinement, joy, and salvation are present in the introduction of 1 Peter as well.

The introduction of 1 Peter opens the narrative world of which the primary story is God's salvation. First Peter 1:3–12 repeats the major elements of the story found in Isa 48–49: refinement (1:7), joy (1:6, 8), and salvation (1:5, 9, 10). Peter encourages his audience to remember the trials they are undergoing have come to prove the genuineness of their faith in order that their faith might result in praise, glory, and honor at Jesus's coming (1:6–7). Moreover, his discussion of the refinement process can be viewed as a development of the "living hope" (1:3) mentioned at the outset of the introduction. The passage in Isaiah certainly corresponds conceptually to the situation of 1 Peter's audience. In both texts there is a group of people who struggle but are encouraged by salvation and God's mission.

Based on the correspondences between 1 Peter and Isa 48–49, the interpretant for this sign-object relation is described best as hope. The role of this initial reference to Isaiah is significant. Not only does this echo key the reader in to the salvation narrative of history, but it also sets up Peter's discussion of the nature of prophecy (1:10–12) and the numerous references to Isaiah that will follow. On the latter point, the subsequent allusions and citations in the epistle strengthen the presence of this intertextual echo in 1 Pet 1:7.

Isaiah 52:3 in 1 Peter 1:18

An allusion to Isa 52:3 can be detected in 1 Pet 1:18. The sign as it appears in 1 Peter shares some linguistic commonalities with the immediate object, as shown in table 12 below.

---

32. In Jewish thought, that one's faith in God was tested by trials as metals were tested by fire was a common belief. See Achtemeier, *1 Peter*, 101–2. He lists the following as support for this: Ps 66:10; Sir 2:5; Prov 17:3; 27:21; Zech 13:9; Mal 3:3; Wis 3:4–6; Jdt 8:25–27; cf. *Herm. Vis.* 4:3, 4.

Defending Hope

Table 12. Isaiah 52:3 in 1 Peter 1:18

1 Peter 1:18	Isaiah 52:3 (OG)
εἰδότες ὅτι οὐ φθαρτοῖς ἀργυρίῳ ἢ χρυσίῳ, ἐλυτρώθητε ἐκ τῆς ματαίας ὑμῶν ἀναστροφῆς πατροπαραδότου	ὅτι τάδε λέγει κύριος δωρεὰν ἐπράθητε καὶ οὐ μετὰ ἀργυρίου λυτρωθήσεσθε

The linguistic links between the two texts are comprised of the verb for "redeem/ransom" and the noun for "money." While ransom language occurs throughout the OT, Isa 52:3 is the only place where ἀργύριον and λυτρόω are found together, thus strengthening this reference as an allusion to Isaiah. The differences in the form of the verb "redeem" can be explained from the differing historical points of view. In the MT and OG, the form of the verb reflects the incompleteness of their "redemption without money" since it has not yet occurred (imperfect in Hebrew, future tense in Greek). In 1 Peter, however, their redemption is stated as fact since it has occurred (aorist tense).

In the larger literary context of the immediate object, Isa 52:1–12 describes the coming salvation of the Lord and predicts the deliverance of the people from exile. This passage immediately precedes the suffering servant song in Isa 52:13—53:12. On the one hand, in most of the instances where redemption or ransom language is used, a price for ransom is not mentioned. On the other hand, only in Isa 52:3 is ransom mentioned in conjunction with a price (though it be the negative phrase "without money"). Moreover, Peter applies this statement to his audience by indicating the exact price of their redemption. First Peter 1:19 continues the thought of the allusion by stating that they were ransomed τιμίῳ αἵματι ... Χριστοῦ, something more precious and costly than either silver or gold. Elliott draws the connection between Isaiah 52 and Isaiah 53 as well: "The fact that the 'blood of Christ' is cited here as the means of redemption points to the influence of a specifically Christian tradition in which the thought of Jesus as vicarious ransom for all (Mark 10:45) was developed through the use of Isa 53, which spoke of the vicarious suffering of the servant of God."[33]

The context of this sign in 1 Peter is the author's initial exhortation to holy living (1:13–21). Peter encourages them to remember the nature of their redemption—its requirement of Jesus's blood—as the basis for conducting themselves in all reverence and respect (1:17). Therefore, the resulting interpretant of the sign-object relation is obedience. Peter's audience should

---

33. Elliott, *1 Peter*, 370.

"Signs" of Hope in 1 Peter

demonstrate holiness out of obedience to God, just as Christ's sacrifice of himself—the price of their redemption—was the ultimate act of obedience.

Isaiah 28:16 in 1 Peter 2:4

Isaiah 28:16 appears as a sign not only in 1 Pet 2:6 (addressed above) but also as a sign in 1 Pet 2:4. The difference between the two is that the former is a citation and the latter is an allusion. In the discussion above on the citation of this Isaianic text, the suggestion was that 2:4 introduces the string of citations found in 2:6–7. Table 13 below shows this initial allusive use of the Isaianic text in 1 Pet 2:4 (cf. with the discussion of the citation and table 5 above).

Table 13. Isaiah 28:16 in 1 Peter 2:4

1 Peter 2:4	Isaiah 28:16 (OG)
πρὸς ὃν προσερχόμενοι λίθον ζῶντα ὑπὸ ἀνθρώπων μὲν ἀποδεδοκιμασμένον παρὰ δὲ θεῷ ἐκλεκτὸν ἔντιμον	διὰ τοῦτο οὕτως λέγει κύριος ἰδοὺ ἐγὼ ἐμβαλῶ εἰς τὰ θεμέλια Σιων λίθον πολυτελῆ ἐκλεκτὸν ἀκρογωνιαῖον ἔντιμον εἰς τὰ θεμέλια αὐτῆς καὶ ὁ πιστεύων ἐπ' αὐτῷ οὐ μὴ καταισχυνθῇ

The verse presents contrasting viewpoints of Christ the "living stone": on the one hand, he is rejected by men, but on the other hand, he is chosen and precious before God.[34] When compared to the sign in 1 Pet 2:6, the allusive reference in 2:4 has only three words in common (stone, chosen, and precious) with the immediate object. Plus, the allusion is not preceded by an introductory formula, as is the case with the citation.

By way of summary, the context of the immediate object (Isa 28:16) is a divine directive to the people of God to abandon the false security offered by foreign nations and return to him. The allusion in 1 Pet 2:4 anticipates the quotation from Isa 28:16; thus, the meaning of the allusion is the same here as the citation in 2:6. Christ is the precious cornerstone and source of honor, not shame, for those who believe in him. Moyise and Menken state the important role of this literary allusion as follows: "Had the full text of Isa. 28:16 been quoted at the beginning, he could not have made

---

34. The relative pronoun ὃν has as its antecedent ὁ κύριος (2:3b). Though 2:3b is a citation of Ps 34:8, "the Lord" here does not refer to God but Christ. This shift in meaning is corroborated by the substitution of κυρίου for θεοῦ in 1:25. Elliott, 403, adds that ὃν also refers forward to Ἰησοῦ Χριστοῦ in 2:5.

the comparison 'like living stones, let yourselves be built into a spiritual house,' for a building is not comprised of numerous cornerstones."[35] Further, this preliminary allusion in 2:4 allows the citation in 2:6 to complete the author's argument, thus giving the citation greater rhetorical effect.[36] The interpretant of hope not only reinforces the string of citations in 2:6–7, but also it provides support for the opening statement of v. 4 as to why they should "come to him" (πρὸς ὃν προσερχόμενοι).

Isaiah 10:3 in 1 Peter 2:12

The second section of the body (2:11—3:12) begins with an allusion to Isa 10:3. First Peter 2:12 contains this sign, as table 14 illustrates.

Table 14. Isaiah 10:3 in 1 Peter 2:12

1 Peter 2:12	Isaiah 10:3 (OG)
τὴν ἀναστροφὴν ὑμῶν ἐν τοῖς ἔθνεσιν ἔχοντες καλήν, ἵνα ἐν ᾧ καταλαλοῦσιν ὑμῶν ὡς κακοποιῶν ἐκ τῶν καλῶν ἔργων ἐποπτεύοντες δοξάσωσιν τὸν θεὸν ἐν ἡμέρᾳ ἐπισκοπῆς.	καὶ τί ποιήσουσιν ἐν τῇ ἡμέρᾳ τῆς ἐπισκοπῆς ἡ γὰρ θλῖψις ὑμῖν πόρρωθεν ἥξει καὶ πρὸς τίνα καταφεύξεσθε τοῦ βοηθηθῆναι καὶ ποῦ καταλείψετε τὴν δόξαν ὑμῶν

While the exact phrase ἐν ἡμέρᾳ ἐπισκοπῆς occurs together only in Isa 10:3 (OG and MT), the reference is deemed an allusion—and not a citation—primarily because similar phrases or concepts occur throughout the OT.[37] One such phrase is the eschatological "day of the Lord," which generally refers to the day of God's judgment (Isa 2:12–21; Amos 5:18–20; Zeph 1:7, 14–15; 2:2–3; Zech 12–14; Mal 4:1–6). Other references to God visiting his people are often ambiguous, having either a positive denotation or a negative denotation. Positive examples include deliverance from Egyptian bondage (Gen 50:21–25; Exod 3:16; 4:31; 13:19) and deliverance from Babylonian captivity (Jer 27:22; 29:10; 32:5; Zech 10:3). Negative examples

---

35. Moyise and Menken, *Isaiah*, 180.

36. See van Rensburg and Moyise, "1 Peter 2:4–10," 22–23, 27. On the allusion to Isa 28:16 in 1 Pet 2:4 they state as follows: "Thus the author has set up both an interpretive framework for understanding the quotations that follow and a rhetorical strategy for increasing their value as proof-texts. Several of the key words have now been used and so when they occur in the explicit quotations, the 'fit' appears more convincing" (23).

37. Peter's omission of the definite articles that are in the OG is insignificant since the article often is omitted in a Greek prepositional phrase.

"Signs" of Hope in 1 Peter

include a coming in judgment (Exod 32:34; Job 6:14; 7:18; Ps 58:6; Jer 6:15; 8:12; 10:5) and a time of testing (Ps 17:3; Job 7:18; 31:14). In addition to these similar phrases and concepts, the allusion is also not clearly marked by any explicit formula. In view of the aforementioned reasons and the definition of an allusion, the intertextual reference is best deemed an allusion.

A cursory reading of the literary context and setting of the immediate object (Isa 10:3) reveals that God's visitation in this case is a negative matter for the people. Isaiah 9:8–10:4 consists of a lengthy woe to Israel, who has turned aside from God's laws and oppressed the poor. Setting the tone for this woe section is the following statement that is repeated four times throughout the passage: "In spite of all this, his anger does not turn away and his hand is still stretched out" (9:12, 17, 21; 10:4). When this context is read alongside the context of 1 Pet 2:11—3:12, the sign seems to be a negative reference to a day of judgment, since this event is mentioned elsewhere in 1 Peter (1:5, 7, 13; 4:7, 13, 17; 5:1).[38]

On the contrary, Elliott argued that the incorporation of the allusion is understood properly in 1 Peter "*as an occasion of testing*" for nonbelievers (cf. 2:12).[39] This understanding is supported by references in the epistle to the present reality of testing (1:6–7; 4:12) and the similar thought of 3:1–2, which indicates the behavior of believing wives might win over their unbelieving husbands. Regarding the author's purpose for incorporating this allusion, Elliott succinctly wrote: "He impresses upon them the hopeful prospect that honorable behavior on their part will not only demonstrate their innocence but can even prompt the conversion of those who malign them."[40] If this understanding is adopted, then the interpretant is one of hope for those who live honorably. Not only can the audience find hope in the God who delivers his people from bondage and suffering, but hope is also found in knowing that their behavior might result in the glorification of God by those who are converted.

---

38. So Achtemeier, *1 Peter*, 178. He stated that "at the time of the final judgment nonbelievers will be brought to the realization that the Christians did what they did at God's behest and with divine approval, and thus be led to glorify God" (178). Also, he pointed out that ἐπισκοπή can mean "blessing"; but when it is used with a temporal designation such as ὥρα, ἡμέρα, or καιρός, it has the connotation of judgment (n. 82).

39. Elliott, *1 Peter*, 471.

40. Ibid.

Defending Hope

Isaiah 53 in 1 Peter 2:23–25

Following the citation of Isa 53:9 in 1 Pet 2:22, at least five allusions to the Suffering Servant song of Isaiah 53 are present. Table 15 below illustrates the various allusions. In the discussion of the citation of Isaiah 53 above, the conclusion reached was that 1 Pet 2:22 supports 2:21 by identifying Christ as the suffering servant, who is the example *par excellence* that the audience (suffering slaves/servants) should follow. The citation also serves as a reference point for the audience as it prepares them for the saturation of allusions that follow. The allusions continue to draw connections between Christ and the Suffering Servant of Isaiah. As a result, the audience is provided a more complete portrait of what endurance in suffering entails. The references here are deemed allusions primarily due to the less explicit linguistic commonalities in comparison to the volume of connections that exist between the citation and its immediate object. In the following analysis, the form of each allusion is addressed in turn. Then a concluding statement of the interpretant is given.

"Signs" of Hope in 1 Peter

Table 15. Isaiah 53 in 1 Peter 2:23-25

1 Peter 2:23	Isaiah 53:7 (OG)
ὃς λοιδορούμενος οὐκ ἀντελοιδόρει, πάσχων οὐκ ἠπείλει, παρεδίδου δὲ τῷ κρίνοντι δικαίως :	καὶ αὐτὸς διὰ τὸ κεκακῶσθαι οὐκ ἀνοίγει τὸ στόμα ὡς πρόβατον ἐπὶ σφαγὴν ἤχθη καὶ ὡς ἀμνὸς ἐναντίον τοῦ κείροντος αὐτὸν ἄφωνος οὕτως οὐκ ἀνοίγει τὸ στόμα αὐτοῦ
1 Peter 2:24	Isaiah 53:4, 5, 12 (OG)
ὃς τὰς ἁμαρτίας ἡμῶν αὐτὸς ἀνήνεγκεν ἐν τῷ σώματι αὐτοῦ ἐπὶ τὸ ξύλον, ἵνα ταῖς ἁμαρτίαις ἀπογενόμενοι τῇ δικαιοσύνῃ ζήσωμεν, οὗ τῷ μώλωπι ἰάθητε.	4 οὗτος τὰς ἁμαρτίας ἡμῶν φέρει καὶ περὶ ἡμῶν ὀδυνᾶται καὶ ἡμεῖς ἐλογισάμεθα αὐτὸν εἶναι ἐν πόνῳ καὶ ἐν πληγῇ καὶ ἐν κακώσει 5 αὐτὸς δὲ ἐτραυματίσθη διὰ τὰς ἀνομίας ἡμῶν καὶ μεμαλάκισται διὰ τὰς ἁμαρτίας ἡμῶν παιδεία εἰρήνης ἡμῶν ἐπ' αὐτόν τῷ μώλωπι αὐτοῦ ἡμεῖς ἰάθημεν 12 διὰ τοῦτο αὐτὸς κληρονομήσει πολλούς καὶ τῶν ἰσχυρῶν μεριεῖ σκῦλα ἀνθ' ὧν παρεδόθη εἰς θάνατον ἡ ψυχὴ αὐτοῦ καὶ ἐν τοῖς ἀνόμοις ἐλογίσθη καὶ αὐτὸς ἁμαρτίας πολλῶν ἀνήνεγκεν καὶ διὰ τὰς ἁμαρτίας αὐτῶν παρεδόθη
1 Peter 2:25	Isaiah 53:6 (OG)
ἦτε γὰρ ὡς πρόβατα πλανώμενοι, ἀλλὰ ἐπεστράφητε νῦν ἐπὶ τὸν ποιμένα καὶ ἐπίσκοπον τῶν ψυχῶν ὑμῶν.	πάντες ὡς πρόβατα ἐπλανήθημεν ἄνθρωπος τῇ ὁδῷ αὐτοῦ ἐπλανήθη καὶ κύριος παρέδωκεν αὐτὸν ταῖς ἁμαρτίαις ἡμῶν

The intertextual sign in 1 Pet 2:23 shares no exact verbal or linguistic similarities with its immediate object (Isa 53:7), though conceptual similarities are present.[41] First, evil is done to the servant in both texts: he was oppressed and afflicted (OG/MT); he was insulted, and he suffered (NT). Second, the emphasis in both texts is the response of silence to such evil actions: the clause "he did not open his mouth" brackets this verse (OG/MT); he did not retaliate, and he did not threaten (NT). Finally, 1 Pet 2:23 shares the passive demeanor which is conveyed in the citation in 2:22. The difference between Isa 53:7 and Isa 53:9 (the citation located in 1 Pet 2:22) is that the

---

41. Achtemeier, *1 Peter*, 200-204, observed that while Peter uses the language of Isaiah 53, the order of references follows the sequence of events in the passion narrative. First Peter 2:22-23 alludes to Jesus's trial, 2:24 alludes to the crucifixion, and 2:25 presupposes the resurrection.

Defending Hope

latter indicates *what* he did not speak ("no deceit was found in his mouth"), whereas the former indicates *that* he did not speak ("he did not retaliate . . . he did not threaten"). Submitting to authorities and masters required, at times, a response not only of silence, but non-retaliation.

First Peter 2:24 begins and ends with allusions. The first part of the verse, τὰς ἁμαρτίας ἡμῶν αὐτὸς ἀνήνεγκεν, finds correspondence in both Isa 53:4 and Isa 53:12. Isaiah 53:4 contains τὰς ἁμαρτίας ἡμῶν, but has the present tense φέρει, as opposed to the aorist tense in 1 Peter. The verbal form is explained when one observes the similarities between the 1 Peter text and Isa 53:12 OG. The latter contains the exact same verb form (ἀνήνεγκεν) and also has the third person pronoun αὐτὸς. Since both Isaianic texts (53:4 and 53:12) explain the reference in 1 Peter, the author likely did not have one or the other in mind, but both. Concluding the verse in 1 Peter is the explanation that "by the wound [of Christ] you were healed." The same wording is found in Isa 53:5 except for the verb form, which the author of 1 Peter changed from first person plural (ἰάθημεν) to second person plural (ἰάθητε) to connect the statement to his audience. While the specific "wound" of Christ is difficult to identify, 2:24 indicates that he bore our sins so that we might be freed from sin.[42]

Finally, 1 Pet 2:25 contains an allusive reference to Isa 53:6. At first glance, this reference appears to be a citation since Peter preserves the same wording as the OG, but with a different form of the verb πλανάω. The reference, however, more properly is deemed an allusion because this same phrase appears also in Isa 13:14 and Ps 119:176. Moreover, there are numerous references in the OT to the people of God being likened to sheep.[43] Peter not only changes the verbal form from first person aorist passive (ἐπλανήθημεν) to present middle participle (πλανώμενοι), but he also adds the second person ἦτε to the participle, resulting in the following reading: "for *you were* like sheep *going astray*." The audience of 1 Peter is likened to the straying flock of

---

42. For a discussion of the identification of the "wound," see Achtemeier, *1 Peter*, 203, nn. 197–98. Achtemeier gave no indication of his position, but concluded "that our author sees in Jesus' death a vicarious suffering by which a new life freed from sin is made possible, a theology already nascent in the description of the suffering servant in Isaiah 53 from which this verse is largely drawn" (203). Additionally, Michaels suggested that Peter intends throughout 2:18–25 not to indicate Christ "died" or was even dead for a short while then rose to life, but that he was "somehow alive through it all, waiting for his straying sheep to return" (*1 Peter*, 150).

43. In the LXX, these references are 2 Chr 18:16; Jdt 11:19; Ps 43:12, 23; 48:15; 76:21; 77:52; 106:41; 118:76; Job 21:11; Mic 2:12; Zech 9:16; 10:2; Isa 53:6–7; and Ezek 36:37–38.

sheep in Isaiah 53, but the verse ends on a positive note by stating they have returned to "the shepherd and overseer" of their souls.[44]

The allusions to Isaiah 53 in these few verses of 1 Peter create a sharply defined image of the suffering Christ as an example to the servants/slaves who are suffering unjustly at the hands of crooked masters (2:18). Part of the struggle for these members of the audience could have been their equation of suffering with God's abandonment.[45] The example of Jesus's suffering, however, indicates just the opposite: his suffering was for the purpose of humanity's redemption. Likewise, the unjust suffering of the audience does not reveal that God has abandoned them; rather, it evidences that God has in fact chosen them.[46] Therefore, hope is the interpretant that best governs both the citation of and the allusions to Isaiah 53 in 1 Pet 2:22–25. Each intertextual sign supports the main exhortation of this larger unit (2:18–25) that slaves are to be submissive to masters (2:18). The suffering slaves can demonstrate obedience to God in their handling of suffering, whether just or unjust.

Summary: Intertextual Entries in the Encyclopedia of 1 Peter

In this final step of the methodology, the intertextual references to Isaiah were examined in light of selected portions of the Petrine encyclopedia. Encyclopedic knowledge aided both the recognition of the intertextual signs and the determination of their communicative function. Results from the intratextual analysis of the previous chapter assisted in providing the framework and narrative world in which the signs are located. A proper understanding of the Isaianic signs contributes to a greater comprehension of the vast Petrine encyclopedia. Thus, elements of the text's universe of discourse and encyclopedia informed the intertextual aspect of the Petrine encyclopedia.

If one were to locate in the (virtual) encyclopedia of 1 Peter the entry entitled *Intertextual References*, what would one find there? One such item would be a discussion on Peter's citation techniques. In this section, one

---

44. Jobes, *1 Peter*, 198, noted that the "shepherd" is identified in Isa 40:10–11 as the Lord. Interestingly, she added that 1 Pet 2:25 could be alluding to Ezek 34:11–13, since the latter also joins shepherding and overseeing in a diaspora context.

45. As Jobes related, "The idea that misfortune indicates divine displeasure was perhaps more prevalent in the ancient world than it is today" (*1 Peter*, 197).

46. Referring to extrabiblical texts, Elliott, *1 Peter*, 530–31, proposes that discipline and suffering were necessary items for training children and that suffering produced knowledge.

would read how Peter utilizes only one introductory formula (2:6), but numerous explicit markers. Another section would detail Peter's dependence on the Greek translation of the OT when citing Scripture. Additionally, one would find a section on the specific references to the OT in 1 Peter, foremost of which would be the volume of references to Isaiah.[47]

In the intratextual investigation, the conclusion reached was that the linguistic signs in 1 Peter are read appropriately through the lens of hope. The study of the Isaianic signs supports this conclusion. All but two (1:18 and 3:14–15) convey a message of hope. Of the thirteen signs examined, the majority is concentrated in the first and second main body sections. The first body section (1:13—2:10) contains six references, and the second body section (2:11—3:12) contains four. The introduction and the third and fourth body sections each contain one. None are present in the prescript or postscript. When the signs are plotted in the syntactic structure of the epistle, it appears that they are saturated in the first half of the epistle to set the foundation for the subsequent ethical exhortations.

A semiotic investigation of the use of Isaiah in 1 Peter demonstrates the integral role of the book of Isaiah in the composition of the epistle. As the dynamic object, the book of Isaiah motivated the generation of numerous Isaianic signs in 1 Peter. The signs all point to one specific aspect of the book of Isaiah, their immediate object, and in doing so create an interpretant. Each interpretant was described in the sections above, and most of these interpretants were determined to communicate the idea of *hope*. While each interpretant communicates in its own right a picture of hope for the audience, the cumulative force of all the interpretants points to a message of hope, one that saturates almost every section of this short epistle.

The results from the intertextual investigation above are compiled and presented in table 16 below. A listing of each of the signs, their immediate objects, and their respective interpretants is tabulated according to the order in which they appear in 1 Peter. Viewing the numerous references to Isaiah as a collective body of signs not only makes a strong case for Isaiah as the major source used by Peter, but it also increases the explanatory power of the argument that he is composing a message of hope. Therefore, the Isaianic signs function as signs of hope in the midst of suffering.

---

47. Peter's brief comments elucidating his theory of prophecy (1:10–12) quite possibly could be a prelude to the numerous references to prophetic literature in this short epistle. For more on this topic, see Moyise, *Evoking Scripture*, 78–95.

"Signs" of Hope in 1 Peter

Table 16. Isaianic Signs in 1 Peter

Sign		Object		Interpretant	
Location	Type of reference	Immediate	Dynamic		
1 Pet 1:7	Echo	Isa 48:10	The book of Isaiah	Hope despite suffering	'Signs' of hope in the midst of suffering
1 Pet 1:18	Allusion	Isa 52:3		Obedience in light of the nature of their redemption	
1 Pet 1:24–25	Quotation	Isa 40:6–8		Hope through the enduring nature of God's word	
1 Pet 2:4	Allusion	Isa 28:16		Hope in Christ as the chosen, precious, and living stone	
1 Pet 2:6	Quotation	Isa 28:16		Hope in Christ the cornerstone	
1 Pet 2:8	Quotation	Isa 8:14		Hope in Christ the stumbling stone	
1 Pet 2:9	Quotation	Isa 43:20–21		Hope in being identified as the elect people of God	
1 Pet 2:12	Allusion	Isa 10:3		Hope for those who live honorably	
1 Pet 2:22	Quotation	Isa 53:9		Hope in Christ to endure suffering	
1 Pet 2:23–25	Allusions	Isa 53:4–7, 12		Hope in Christ to endure suffering	
1 Pet 3:14–15	Quotation	Isa 8:12–13		Boldness in the face of suffering	
1 Pet 4:14	Quotation	Isa 11:2		Comfort, hope, and blessing through the Spirit	

Another intriguing insight that can be gained from this semiotic approach is how Peter uses implicit methods for communicating a message of hope. The use of explicit verbal or nominal forms of "hope" is minimal (five total) when compared to the numerous intertextual connections tabulated above (twelve total).[48] In 1 Pet 3:15, Peter encourages his audience to be ready at all times to give a defense (ἀπολογία) of the hope they have in them. In his use of intertextual references to Isaiah, Peter exemplifies how to provide a defense of hope. This defense is rooted in God's dealings with his people

---

48. The explicit occurrences include three nominal forms (from ἐλπίς; 1:3, 21; 3:15) and two verbal forms (from ἐλπίζω; 1:13; 3:5).

and it centers around the portrait of hope that is supplied by Isaiah. Peter's method for evoking this message points to the pragmatic value of the larger story that comprises the background of Isaiah. Moreover, his implicit references to the book of Isaiah demonstrate his assumption that his audience is familiar, if not conversant, with the story of hope narrated by Isaiah.

In conclusion, *meaning* was defined in chapter 2 as Peirce's conception of the interpretant. If the interpretant is the further sign or idea created by the sign-object interaction, then meaning can be described as the translation of a sign into another sign-system. In 1 Peter, the book of Isaiah (dynamic object) supplied the motivation for the author to incorporate Isaianic references (signs) in the construction of his epistle. These intertextual references—which point to specific parts of Isaiah (immediate object)—were created in order to evoke a specific image or idea (interpretant) in the audience's mind, that of hope in suffering. With the incorporation of numerous Isaianic references, the author of 1 Peter effectually creates a sign-system of hope rooted in the book of Isaiah.

Conclusion

BIBLICAL INTERTEXTUALITY IS A branch of textual study that will continue to attract the attention of biblical scholars for years to come. With no agreed-upon methodology to perform such studies, practitioners of intertextuality will continue to adopt varying approaches in examining all forms of scriptural references. The purpose of this study was to explore the use of semiotics as an overarching method for biblical intertextual studies. After a survey of relevant research in chapter 1, a semiotic theory of textuality was delineated and the two major pillars of semiotic theory (universe of discourse and encyclopedia) were examined in turn in chapter 2. Using 1 Peter as the test case, the final three chapters investigated each theoretical construct. Chapter 3 followed Alkier's intratextual approach, which reconstructs a document's universe of discourse by analyzing elements of syntactics, semantics, and pragmatics. Then, chapter 4 addressed the pertinent issues for opening the encyclopedia of 1 Peter. This provided the proper context for examining each intertextual reference to Isaiah in chapter 5.

One result of the investigation was that a semiotic approach to the Isaianic references in 1 Peter does assist in determining their function. Additionally, the majority of the intertextual references provides a message of hope to the suffering audience. Intertextual references to Isaiah (one example of a linguistic sign) are created to communicate something about the book of Isaiah (the dynamic object). The linguistic sign and its object (a specific portion of Isaiah) produce an interpretant, which is the vehicle for carrying the sign's meaning. A semiotic approach also informs the intertextual relationships by requiring a construction of the text's universe and its encyclopedic knowledge, both of which govern the meaning of a sign in a text.

Semiotics has numerous benefits not only for intertextual study, but also for NT and biblical study as a whole. Traditional disciplinary boundaries in NT study are unnecessary limitations to textual approaches and should be minimized as much as possible. A semiotic method is a viable option for allowing the utilization of multiple approaches. One of Alkier's main convictions for employing this method is that it "offers biblical studies the possibility of a common theoretical basis for all subjects of investigation and interpretive processes."[1] In the present study, this point was confirmed as other methodological approaches were naturally incorporated at various points in the investigation. Thus, the elusive discipline of intertextuality is tamed by placing it within a clearly defined realm of textual investigation that is bound to the common theoretical basis of semiotic theory. The binding nature of a semiotic approach is its primary strength. On the other hand, the primary weakness of this method is that it does not resolve or even broach the terminological issue.

A uniqueness of this study is the implementation of an intertextual method that is grounded in both the genesis of the term in secular literary studies (Kristeva et al.) and a distinct philosophical framework (Peirce). The method is not a reaction to where contemporary literary studies have landed—the death of the author. Rather, a semiotic intertextual method demonstrates that the use of such a method does not necessitate the death of the author. Semiotics need not be equated with reader-response approaches or the suppression of historical questions. In fact, Alkier's proposed method acknowledges the viability of the historical-critical method and even allows for a semiotic investigation based upon this approach, though he is negative toward it. A better approach to the perennial problem of intertextual methodology is to combine both historical approaches and intertextual theory, and this combination is aided by the semiotic theory espoused here.[2] In other words, a semiotic approach allows for the strengths of both approaches to come to bear on the text instead of pitting them against one another.

Several areas of further research can be noted as a result of this study. First, an extratextual perspective can be applied to the text of 1 Peter, which would broaden the study to include semiotic insights from textual and literature history, archaeology, cultural anthropology, and social and economic policy. In contrast to textuality and intertextuality, texts are utilized strictly as data sources. An extratextual perspective would enhance

---

1. Alkier, "New Testament Studies," 224.

2. Moyise, "Intertextuality," in *Reading the Bible Intertextually*, 32, argued this same point regarding intertextual methodology.

Conclusion

one's knowledge of the text's encyclopedia. Second, the intertextual analysis could be expanded by examining the experimental form of unlimited intertextuality. For 1 Peter, one could engage in experimental intertextuality by reading the book of Isaiah alongside the Epistle of 1 Peter in the interest of determining which effects of meaning result. In this approach—to follow the proposition of Alkier—the whole book of Isaiah becomes the encyclopedic assumption for what is contained in 1 Peter. Further, 1 Peter becomes the continuation of Isaiah.[3]

A third area of further research would involve the application of speech-act theory to the pragmatic elements of the method. At least a few individuals mentioned in this study have suggested this as an avenue that needs development. In his discussion of the application of semiotic theory, Eco warned that the value of speech-act theory for explaining pragmatic phenomena should not be underestimated.[4] Dryden's work on theology and ethics in 1 Peter is a skillful example of a pragmatic study influenced by speech-act theory; however, his work is indebted more to rhetorical and social-scientific theories than to speech-act theory.[5] In addition, Thiselton has discussed this theory and its application in numerous places, all of which serve as a reasoned approach to studying texts as speech-acts.[6] Thus, an examination of textual features through the lens of speech-act theory would be quite valuable.

Finally, and as with any newer methodology, this semiotic method needs to be applied to other portions of Scripture. For instance, one can examine the intertextual references to the OT in Romans or even the plethora of allusions and echoes in the book of Revelation. In the area of OT intertextuality, one could examine how Isaiah uses Torah. One also could perform an intratextual investigation of the Gospel of John, which incorporates a narrative-critical approach. The value of this method can be seen on a larger level only after significant application of it to other portions of Scripture.

In conclusion, biblical intertextuality remains an extremely complex discipline. The complexity might well explain the multitude of methodological approaches to the intertextual references in Scripture. Acknowledging

---

3. The work by Watts on Mark's use of Isaiah resembles this type of approach (*Isaiah's New Exodus*). Watts's work would be an excellent point of comparison for those who engage in an experimental form of intertextual study.
4. Eco, *The Limits of Interpretation*, 48.
5. Dryden, *Theology and Ethics*, 10–12.
6. See Thiselton's detailed comments in *New Horizons*.

these issues, Moyise states, "this complexity is best served by combining a number of approaches rather than fastening on just one. Evoking Scripture 'opens up' rather than 'closes down' and our methods of study need to be sensitive to this."[7] In effect, Moyise is calling for an interdisciplinary approach to this field of study. While methods will come and go, the firm conviction of this author is that an engagement with semiotics will push the scholarly community closer to an established method for studying the intertextuality of biblical literature. Hopefully, such an approach will assist in navigating the rocky terrain of intertextual studies and afford the opportunity for new directions in intertextual research.

---

7. Moyise, *Evoking Scripture*, 141.

Bibliography

Achtemeier, Elizabeth. *The Community and Message of Isaiah 56-66: A Theological Commentary*. Minneapolis: Augsburg, 1982.
Achtemeier, Paul J. *1 Peter: A Commentary on First Peter*. Hermeneia. Minneapolis: Fortress, 1996.
Aichele, George, and Gary Phillips. "Introduction: Exegesis, Eisegesis, Intergesis." *Semeia* 69 (1995) 7-18.
Alkier, Stefan. "From Text to Intertext: Intertextuality as a Paradigm for Reading Matthew." *Hervormde teologiese studies* 61 (2005) 1-18.
———. "Intertextuality and the Semiotics of Biblical Texts." In *Reading the Bible Intertextually*, edited by Richard B. Hays, Stefan Alkier, and Leroy A. Huizenga, 3-21. Waco, TX: Baylor University Press, 2009.
———. New Testament Studies on the Basis of Categorical Semiotics." In *Reading the Bible Intertextually*, edited by Richard B. Hays, Stefan Alkier, and Leroy A. Huizenga, 223-48. Waco, TX: Baylor University Press, 2009.
———. *Wunder und Wirklichkeit in den Briefen des Apostels Paulus: Ein Beitrag zu einem Wunderverständnis jenseits von Entmythologisierung und Re-historisierung*. Wissenschaftliche Untersuchungen zum Neuen Testament 134. Tübingen: Mohr Siebeck, 2001.
Allen, Graham. *Intertextuality*. The New Critical Idiom. London: Routledge, 2000.
Almeder, Robert. *The Philosophy of Charles S. Peirce: A Critical Introduction*. Totowa, NJ: Rowman and Littlefield, 1980.
Apel, Karl-Otto. *Charles S. Peirce: From Pragmatism to Pragmaticism*. Translated by John Michael Krois. Amherst: University of Massachusetts Press, 1981.
Archer, Gleason L., and Gregory Chirichigno. *Old Testament Quotations in the New Testament*. Eugene, OR: Wipf & Stock, 2005.
Bains, Paul. *The Primacy of Semiosis: An Ontology of Relations*. Toronto: University of Toronto Press, 2006.
Bakhtin, Mikhail. *The Dialogic Imagination*. Edited by Michael Holquist. Translated by Caryl Emerson and Michael Holquist. Austin: University of Texas Press, 1981.
Bally, C., and A. Sechehaye, editors. *Cours de linguistique générale*. Paris: Payot, 1916. Translated by W. Baskin as *Course in General Linguistics*. New York: McGraw-Hill, 1958.
Baltzer, Klaus. *Deutero-Isaiah: A Commentary on Isaiah 40-55*. Hermeneia. Minneapolis: Fortress, 2001.

Bibliography

Barthes, Roland. *Elements of Semiology*. Translated by Annette Lavers and Colin Smith. New York: Hill and Wang, 1967.

———. *S/Z*. Translated by Richard Miller. New York: Hill and Wang, 1974.

Beale, Gregory K., editor. *The Right Doctrine from the Wrong Text: Essays on the Use of the Old Testament in the New*. Grand Rapids: Baker Books, 1994.

Beale, G. K., and D. A. Carson, editors. *Commentary on the New Testament Use of the Old Testament*. Grand Rapids: Baker Academic, 2007.

Beckwith, Roger. *The Old Testament Canon of the New Testament Church and Its Background in Early Judaism*. Grand Rapids: Eerdmans, 1985.

Ben-Porat, Ziva. "The Poetics of Literary Allusion." *PTL: A Journal for Descriptive Poetics and Theory of Literature* 1 (1976) 105–28.

Bernstein, Richard J. *Perspectives on Peirce: Critical Essays on Charles Sanders Peirce*. New Haven: Yale University Press, 1965.

Boismard, Marie-Émile. *Quatre hymnes baptismales dans la Première Épître de Pierre*. Paris: Cerf, 1961.

Boole, George. *An Investigation of the Laws of Thought*. Cambridge: Macmillan, 1854.

Boring, M. Eugene. *1 Peter*. Abingdon New Testament Commentaries. Nashville: Abingdon Press, 1999.

Brent, Joseph. *Charles Sanders Peirce: A Life*. Revised and enlarged edition. Bloomington: Indiana University Press, 1998.

Brodie, Thomas L., Dennis R. MacDonald, and Stanley E. Porter, editors. *The Intertextuality of the Epistles: Explorations of Theory and Practice*. Sheffield: Sheffield Phoenix Press, 2006.

Buchanan, George Wesley. *Introduction to Intertextuality*. Lewiston, NY: Mellen Biblical, 1994.

Buchler, Justus, editor. *Philosophical Writings of Peirce*. New York: Dover, 1955.

Burks, Arthur W., editor. *Collected Papers of Charles Sanders Peirce*. Vol, 8, *Reviews, Correspondence, and Bibliography*. Cambridge, MA: Harvard University Press, 1958.

Campbell, Barth L. *Honor, Shame, and the Rhetoric of 1 Peter*. SBL Dissertation Series 160. Atlanta: Scholars, 1998.

Carson, D. A., and H. G. M. Williamson, editors. *It Is Written: Scripture Citing Scripture: Essays in Honor of Barnabas Lindars*. Cambridge: Cambridge University Press, 1988.

Chandler, Daniel. *Semiotics: The Basics*. 2nd. ed. London: Routledge, 2007.

Childs, Brevard S. *Isaiah*. The Old Testament Library. Louisville: Westminster John Knox, 2001.

Clark, H. H., and R. R. Gerrig. "Quotations as Demonstrations." *Language* 66 (1990) 767–93.

Clarke, D. S. *Principles of Semiotic*. London: Routledge and Kegan Paul, 1987.

Classen, Carl Joachim. *Rhetorical Criticism of the New Testament*. Wissenschaftliche Untersuchungen zum Neuen Testament 128. Tübingen: Mohr Siebeck, 2000.

Clayton, Jay, and Eric Rothstein, editors. *Influence and Intertextuality in Literary History*. Madison: University of Wisconsin Press, 1991.

Cobley, Paul, and Litza Jansz. *Introducing Semiotics: A Graphic Guide*. London: Icon Books, 2010.

Copeland, James E., editor. *New Directions in Linguistics and Semiotics*. Houston: Rice University Press, 1984.

Bibliography

Corrington, Robert S. *The Community of Interpreters: On the Hermeneutics of Nature and the Bible in the American Philosophical Tradition*. Studies in American Biblical Hermeneutics 3. Macon, GA: Mercer University Press, 1987.

———. *A Semiotic Theory of Theology and Philosophy*. Cambridge: Cambridge University Press, 2000.

Corti, Maria. *An Introduction to Literary Semiotics*. Translated by Margherita Bogat and Allen Mandelbaum. Bloomington: Indiana University Press, 1978.

Cross, F. L. *1 Peter: A Paschal Liturgy*. London: Mowbray, 1954.

Culler, Jonathan. *The Pursuit of Signs: Semiotics, Literature, Deconstruction*. Ithaca, NY: Cornell University Press, 1981.

Danesi, Marcel. *Messages and Meanings: An Introduction to Semiotics*. Toronto: Canadian Scholars Press, 1994.

———. *The Quest for Meaning: A Guide to Semiotic Theory and Practice*. Toronto: University of Toronto Press, 2007.

Davids, Peter H. *The First Epistle of Peter*. New International Commentary on the New Testament. Grand Rapids: Eerdmans, 1990.

De Morgan, Augustus. "On the Syllogism, I: On the Structure of the Syllogism." *Transactions of the Cambridge Philosophical Society* 8 (1846) 379–403.

de Waal, Cornelius. *On Peirce*. Wadsworth Philosophers Series. Belmont, CA: Wadsworth Thomson Learning, 2001.

Deely, John. *Basics of Semiotics*. Bloomington: Indiana University Press, 1990.

———. "Toward the Origin of Semiotic." In *Sight, Sound, and Sense*, edited by Thomas A. Sebeok, 1–30. Bloomington, IN: Indiana University Press, 1978.

Deledalle, Gérard. *Charles S. Peirce's Philosophy of Signs: Essays in Comparative Semiotics*. Bloomington: Indiana University Press, 2000.

Derrida, Jacques. "Living On: Border Lines." In *Deconstruction and Criticism*, edited by Harold Bloom, 75–176. New York: Seabury, 1979.

Dodd, C. H. *According to the Scriptures: The Sub-Structure of New Testament Theology*. London: Nisbet & Co., 1952.

Donelson, Lewis R. *I & II Peter and Jude: A Commentary*. New Testament Library. Louisville: Westminster John Knox, 2010.

Dryden, J. de Waal. *Theology and Ethics in 1 Peter: Paraenetic Strategies for Christian Character Formation*. Wissenschaftliche Untersuchungen zum Neuen Testament 209. Tübingen: Mohr Siebeck, 2006.

Dubis, Mark. *Messianic Woes in First Peter: Suffering and Eschatology in 1 Peter 4:12–19*. Studies in Biblical Literature 33. New York: Peter Lang, 2002.

———. "Research on 1 Peter: A Survey of Scholarly Literature Since 1985." *Currents in Biblical Research* 4 (2006) 199–239.

Duhm, Bernhard. *Das Buch Jesaia*. Handkommentar zum Alten Testament. Göttingen: Vandenhoeck & Ruprecht, 1892.

Dunning, Benjamin H. "Aliens and Sojourners: Self as Other in the Rhetoric of Early Christian Identity." PhD diss., Harvard University, 2005.

Eco, Umberto. *The Limits of Interpretation*. Bloomington: Indiana University Press, 1990.

———. *The Role of the Reader: Exploration in the Semiotics of Texts*. Bloomington: Indiana University Press, 1979.

———. *Semiotics and the Philosophy of Language*. Bloomington: Indiana University Press, 1984.

———. *A Theory of Semiotics*. Bloomington: Indiana University Press, 1976.

Bibliography

Eco, Umberto, and Costantino Marmo, editors. *On the Medieval Theory of Signs*. Amsterdam: John Benjamins, 1989.

Elliott, John H. *The Elect and the Holy*. Supplements to Novum Testamentum 12. Leiden: Brill, 1966.

———. *1 Peter: A New Translation with Introduction and Commentary*. The Anchor Bible Series. Vol. 37B. New York: Doubleday, 2000.

———. *A Home for the Homeless: A Social-Scientific Criticism of I Peter, Its Situation and Strategy*. Eugene, OR: Wipf & Stock, 1990.

———. "The Rehabilitation of an Exegetical Step-Child: 1 Peter in Recent Research." *Journal of Biblical Literature* 95 (1976) 243–54.

Ellis, E. Earle. *The Old Testament in Early Christianity: Canon and Interpretation in the Light of Modern Research*. Wissenschaftliche Untersuchungen zum Neuen Testament 54. Tübingen: Mohr Siebeck, 1991. Reprint, Eugene, OR: Wipf & Stock, 2003.

Ellul, Danielle. "Un exemple de cheminement rhétorique: 1 Pierre." *Revue d'histoire et de philosophie religieuses* 70 (1990) 17–34.

Ericson, Norman R. "The NT Use of the OT: A Kerygmatic Approach." *Journal of the Evangelical Theological Society* 30 (1987) 337–42.

Evans, Craig A. *Ancient Texts for New Testament Studies: A Guide to the Background Literature*. Peabody, MA: Hendrickson, 2005.

———, editor. *From Prophecy to Testament: The Function of the Old Testament in the New*. Peabody, MA: Hendrickson, 2004.

Evans, Craig A., and James A. Sanders, editors. *Early Christian Interpretation of the Scriptures of Israel: Investigations and Proposals*. Journal for the Study of the New Testament Supplement Series 148. Sheffield: Sheffield Academic, 1997.

Evans, Craig A., and W. Richard Stegner. *The Gospels and the Scriptures of Israel*. Journal for the Study of the New Testament Supplement Series 104. Sheffield: Sheffield Academic Press, 1994.

Evans, Craig A., and William F. Stinespring, editors. *Early Jewish and Christian Exegesis: Studies in Memory of William Hugh Brownlee*. Atlanta: Scholars, 1987.

Evans, Craig A., and Shemaryahu Talmon, editors. *The Quest for Context and Meaning: Studies in Biblical Intertextuality in Honor of James A. Sanders*. Leiden: Brill, 1997.

Feldmeier, Reinhard. *The First Letter of Peter: A Commentary on the Greek Text*. Translated by Peter H. Davids. Waco, TX: Baylor University Press, 2008.

Fewell, Danna Nolan, editor. *Reading Between Texts: Intertextuality and the Hebrew Bible*. Louisville: Westminster John Knox, 1992.

Fisch, Max H., editor. *Classic American Philosophers*. 2nd ed. New York: Fordham University Press, 1996.

———, editor. *Writings of Charles S. Peirce: A Chronological Edition*. Vol. 1, *1857–1866*. Bloomington: Indiana University Press, 1982.

Fitzgerald, John J. *Peirce's Theory of Signs as Foundation for Pragmatism*. Studies in Philosophy 11. The Hague: Mouton & Co., 1966.

Fitzmyer, J. A. "The Use of Explicit Old Testament Quotations in Qumran Literature and in the New Testament." *New Testament Studies* 7 (1960) 299–305.

Forest, Michael J. "Charles S. Peirce: Truth, Reality and Objective Semiotic Idealism." PhD diss., Marquette University, 2000.

Frawley, William. "In Defence of the Dictionary: A Response to Haiman." *Lingua* 55 (1981) 53–61.

Bibliography

Gardner, Howard. *The Quest for Mind: Piaget, Lévi-Strauss, and the Structuralist Movement.* 2nd ed. Chicago: University of Chicago Press, 1981.

George, George Anthony. "Charles S. Peirce's Development of Semiotics from Logic and Pragmatism to a Concept of God." PhD diss., Florida State University, 2000.

Glenny, W. Edward. "The Hermeneutics of the Use of the Old Testament in 1 Peter." ThD diss., Dallas Theological Seminary, 1987.

Goldingay, John. *Isaiah.* New International Biblical Commentary 13. Peabody, MA: Hendrickson, 2001.

Goppelt, Leonhard. *A Commentary on 1 Peter.* Göttingen: Vandenhoech & Ruprecht, 1978. English edition. Translated by John E. Alsup. Grand Rapids: Eerdmans, 1993.

———. *Typos: The Typological Interpretation of the Old Testament in the New.* Translated by Donald H. Madvig. Grand Rapids: Eerdmans, 1981.

Gréaux, Eric James. "'To the Elect Exiles of the Dispersion . . . from Babylon': The Function of the Old Testament in 1 Peter." PhD diss., Duke University, 2003.

Green, Gene L. "The Use of the Old Testament for Christian Ethics in 1 Peter." *Tyndale Bulletin* 41 (1990) 276–89.

Green, Joel B., editor. *Hearing the New Testament: Strategies for Interpretation.* 2nd ed. Grand Rapids: Eerdmans, 2010.

Grudem, Wayne A. *1 Peter.* Tyndale New Testament Commentary. Grand Rapids: Eerdmans, 1988.

Gundry, R. H. "'Verba Christi' in 1 Peter: Their Implications concerning the Authorship of 1 Peter and the Authenticity of the Gospel Tradition." *New Testament Studies* 13 (1966) 336–50.

Haiman, John. "Dictionaries and Encyclopedias." *Lingua* 50 (1980) 329–57.

———. "Dictionaries and Encyclopedias Again." *Lingua* 56 (1982) 353–55.

Hall, Sean. *This Means This, This Means That: A User's Guide to Semiotics.* London: Laurence King, 2007.

Hanson, Anthony T. *The New Testament Interpretation of Scripture.* London: SPCK, 1980.

Hardwick, Charles S., editor. *Semiotic and Significs: The Correspondence between Charles S. Peirce and Victoria Lady Welby.* Bloomington: Indiana University Press, 1977.

Hartshorne, Charles, and Paul Weiss, editors. *Collected Papers of Charles Sanders Peirce.* Vol. 5, *Pragmatism and Pragmaticism.* Vol. 6, *Scientific Metaphysics.* Cambridge, MA: Belknap Press of Harvard University Press, 1960.

Hatina, Thomas R. "Intertextuality and Historical Criticism in New Testament Studies: Is There a Relationship?" *Biblical Interpretation* 7 (1999) 28–43.

Hawkes, Terence. *Structuralism and Semiotics.* 2nd ed. London: Routledge, 2003.

Hays, Richard B. "Can the Gospels Teach Us How to Read the Old Testament?" *Pro Ecclesia* 11 (2002) 402–18.

———. *The Conversion of the Imagination: Paul as Interpreter of Israel's Scripture.* Grand Rapids: Eerdmans, 2005.

———. "The Conversion of the Imagination: Scripture and Eschatology in 1 Corinthians." *New Testament Studies* 45 (1999) 391–412.

———. *Echoes of Scripture in the Letters of Paul.* New Haven, CT: Yale University Press, 1989.

———. *The Faith of Jesus Christ: An Investigation of the Narrative Substructure of Galatians 3:1–4:11.* Society of Biblical Literature Dissertation Series 56. Chico, CA: Scholars, 1983.

Bibliography

Hays, Richard B., Stefan Alkier, and Leroy A. Huizenga, editors. *Reading the Bible Intertextually*. Waco, TX: Baylor University Press, 2009.

Hillyer, Norman. *1 and 2 Peter, Jude*. New International Biblical Commentary. Peabody, MA: Hendrickson, 1992.

Houser, Nathan, editor. *The Essential Peirce: Selected Philosophical Writings*. Vol. 2, 1893-1913. Bloomington: Indiana University Press, 1998.

———, editor. *Writings of Charles S. Peirce: A Chronological Edition*. Vol. 6, 1886-1890. Bloomington: Indiana University Press, 2000.

Houser, Nathan, and Christian Kloesel, editors. *The Essential Peirce: Selected Philosophical Writings*. Vol. 1, 1867-1893. Bloomington: Indiana University Press, 1992.

Hübner, Hans. "Quotations in the New Testament." In *The Anchor Bible Dictionary*, edited by David Noel Freedman, 1096-1104. Translated by Siegfried S. Schatzmann. Vol. 4. New York: Doubleday, 1992.

Huizenga, Leroy A. "The Matthean Jesus and the Isaac of the Early Jewish Encyclopedia." In *Reading the Bible Intertextually*, edited by Richard B. Hays, Stefan Alkier, and Leroy A. Huizenga, 63-81. Waco, TX: Baylor University Press, 2009.

Innis, Robert E., editor. *Semiotics: An Introductory Anthology*. Bloomington: Indiana University Press, 1985.

Jauhiainen, Marko. *The Use of Zechariah in Revelation*. Wissenschaftliche Untersuchungen zum Neuen Testament 199. Tübingen: Mohr Siebeck, 2005.

Jauss, Hans Robert. *Toward an Aesthetic of Reception*. Translated by Timothy Bahti. Minneapolis: University of Minnesota Press, 1982.

Jobes, Karen H. *1 Peter*. Baker Exegetical Commentary on the New Testament. Grand Rapids: Baker Academic, 2005.

Jobes, Karen H., and Moisés Silva. *Invitation to the Septuagint*. Grand Rapids: Baker Academic, 2000.

Jones, Judith A. "Building on the Rejected Stone: The Metaphorical Construals of Psalm 118:22 in the New Testament." PhD diss., Emory University, 1999.

Juel, Donald. *Messianic Exegesis: Christological Interpretation of the Old Testament in Early Christianity*. Philadelphia: Fortress, 1988.

Kaiser, Walter C. *The Use of the Old Testament in the New*. Chicago: Moody, 1985.

Kennedy, George A. *New Testament Interpretation through Rhetorical Criticism*. Chapel Hill: University of North Carolina Press, 1984.

Ketner, Kenneth Laine. *His Glassy Essence: An Autobiography of Charles Sanders Peirce*. Nashville: Vanderbilt University Press, 1998.

Klauck, Hans-Josef. *Ancient Letters and the New Testament: A Guide to Context and Exegesis*. Waco, TX: Baylor University Press, 2006.

Klausli, Markus T. "The Question of the Messianic Woes in 1 Peter." PhD diss., Dallas Theological Seminary, 2007.

Kloesel, Christian J. W., editor. *Writings of Charles S. Peirce: A Chronological Edition*. Vol. 4, 1879-1884. Bloomington: Indiana University Press, 1989.

Koch, Dietrich-Alex. "The Quotations of Isaiah 8:14 and 28:16 in Romans 9:33 and 1 Peter 2:6-8 as Test Case for Old Testament Quotations in the New Testament." *Zeitschrift für die neutestamentliche Wissenschaft und die Kunde der Älteren Kirche* 101 (2010) 223-40.

Kristeva, Julia. *Desire in Language: A Semiotic Approach to Literature and Art*. Edited by Leon S. Roudiez. Translated by Thomas Gora, Alice Jardine, and Leon S. Roudiez. New York: Columbia University Press, 1980.

———. *Revolution in Poetic Language*. Translated by Margaret Waller. New York: Columbia University Press, 1984.

———. *Séméiotikè: Recherches pour une sémanalyse*. Collections Tel Quel. Paris: Le Seuil, 1969.

Kwon, Hyukjung. "The Reception of Psalm 118 in the New Testament: Application of a 'New Exodus Motif?'" PhD diss., University of Pretoria, 2007.

Laato, Antti. *History and Ideology in the Old Testament Prophetic Literature: A Semiotic Approach to the Reconstruction of the Proclamation of Historical Prophets*. Coniectanea Biblica Old Testament Series 41. Stockholm: Almqwist & Wiksell International, 1996.

Lai, Kenny Ke-Chung. "The Holy Spirit in 1 Peter: A Study of Petrine Pneumatology in Light of the Isaianic New Exodus." PhD diss., Dallas Theological Seminary, 2009.

Lea, Thomas D. "How Peter Learned the Old Testament." *Southwestern Journal of Theology* 22 (1980) 96–102.

———. "Peter's Use of the Old Testament." PhD diss., Southwestern Baptist Theological Seminary, 1968.

Lidov, David. *Elements of Semiotics*. New York: St. Martin's, 1999.

Lieb, Irwin, editor. *Charles S. Peirce's Letters to Lady Welby*. New Haven, CT: Whitlock's, 1953.

Lindars, Barnabas. *New Testament Apologetic: The Doctrinal Significance of the Old Testament Quotations*. Philadelphia: Westminster, 1961.

———. "Old Testament Quotations in the New Testament." In *The HarperCollins Bible Dictionary*, edited by Paul J. Achtemeier, 778–81. New York: HarperCollins, 1996.

———. "The Place of the Old Testament in the Formation of New Testament Theology." *New Testament Studies* 23 (1977) 59–75.

Liszka, James Jakób. *A General Introduction to the Semiotic of Charles Sanders Peirce*. Bloomington: Indiana University Press, 1996.

Longenecker, Richard N. *Biblical Exegesis in the Apostolic Period*. 2nd ed. Grand Rapids: Eerdmans, 1999.

Loughlin, Gerard. *Telling God's Story: Bible, Church and Narrative Theology*. Cambridge: Cambridge University Press, 1996.

Mack, Burton L. *Rhetoric and the New Testament*. Guides to Biblical Scholarship. New Testament Series. Minneapolis: Fortress, 1990.

Malherbe, Abraham J. *Ancient Epistolary Theorists*. Atlanta: Scholars, 1988.

Markus, R. A. *Signs and Meanings: World and Text in Ancient Christianity*. 2nd ed. Eugene, OR: Wipf & Stock, 2011.

Marshall, I. Howard. *1 Peter*. The IVP New Testament Commentary. Downers Grove, IL: InterVarsity, 1991.

Martin, R. M. *Semiotics and Linguistic Structure: A Primer of Philosophic Logic*. Albany: State University of New York Press, 1978.

Martin, Troy W. *Metaphor and Composition in 1 Peter*. Society of Biblical Literature Dissertation Series 131. Atlanta: Scholars Press, 1992.

Mbuvi, Andrew M. "Temple, Exile and Identity in 1 Peter." PhD diss., Westminster Theological Seminary, 2004.

McCartney, Dan G. "The Use of the Old Testament in the First Epistle of Peter." PhD diss., Westminster Theological Seminary, 1989.

McDonald, Lee Martin, and James A. Sanders, editors. *The Canon Debate*. Peabody, MA: Hendrickson, 2002.

Bibliography

McKnight, Scot, and Grant R. Osborne, editors. *The Face of New Testament Studies: A Survey of Recent Research.* Grand Rapids: Baker Academic, 2004.

Metzger, Bruce M. "The Formulas Introducing Quotations of Scripture in the NT and the Mishnah." *JBL* 70 (1951) 297–307.

Michaels, J. Ramsey. *1 Peter.* Word Biblical Commentary 49. Nashville: Thomas Nelson, 1988.

Misak, Cheryl, editor. *The Cambridge Companion to Peirce.* Cambridge: Cambridge University Press, 2004.

Mitrik, Robert M. "Literary Semiotics as a Philosophy of Language in the Novels of Umberto Eco." DA thesis, Idaho State University, 2009.

Moi, Toril, editor. *The Kristeva Reader.* New York: Columbia University Press, 1986.

Moore, Edward C. *American Pragmatism: Peirce, James, and Dewey.* New York: Columbia University Press, 1961.

Moore, Stephen D. *Poststructuralism and the New Testament: Derrida and Foucault at the Foot of the Cross.* Minneapolis: Fortress, 1994.

Morris, Charles W. *Foundations of the Theory of Signs.* International Encyclopedia of Unified Science. Vol. 1. Chicago: University of Chicago Press, 1938.

———. *Signs, Language and Behavior.* New York: Prentice-Hall, 1946.

———. *Writings on the General Theory of Signs.* Approaches to Semiotics 16. Edited by Thomas A. Sebeok. The Hague: Mouton, 1971.

Mounce, Robert H. *A Living Hope: A Commentary on 1 and 2 Peter.* Grand Rapids: Eerdmans, 1982.

Moyise, Steve. "Can We Use the New Testament in the Way Which the New Testament Authors Use the Old Testament?" *Die Skriflig* 36 (2002) 643–60.

———. *Evoking Scripture: Seeing the Old Testament in the New.* London: T. & T. Clark, 2008.

———. "Intertextuality and Biblical Studies: A Review." *Verbum et Ecclesia* 23 (2002) 418–31.

———. *The Old Testament in the New: An Introduction.* New York: Continuum, 2001.

———. "Scripture in the New Testament: Literary and Theological Perspectives." *Neotestamentica* 42 (2008) 305–26.

———. "Singing the Song of Moses and the Lamb: John's Dialogical Use of Scripture." *Andrews University Seminary Studies* 42 (2004) 347–60.

———. "The Use of Analogy in Biblical Studies." *Anvil* 18 (2001) 33–42.

Moyise, Steve, and Maarten J. J. Menken, editors. *Isaiah in the New Testament.* London: T. & T. Clark, 2005.

Mulder, Martin Jan, editor. *Mikra: Text, Translation, Reading & Interpretation of the Hebrew Bible in Ancient Judaism & Early Christianity.* Peabody, MA: Hendrickson, 1988.

———. "The Transmission of the Biblical Text." In *Mikra: Text, Translation, Reading & Interpretation of the Hebrew Bible in Ancient Judaism & Early Christianity*, edited by Martin Jan Mulder, 87–136. Peabody, MA: Hendrickson, 1988.

Mullin, Richard P. *The Soul of Classical American Philosophy: The Ethical and Spiritual Insights of William James, Josiah Royce, and Charles Sanders Peirce.* Albany: State University of New York Press, 2007.

Murphy, Roland E. "The Relationship between the Testaments." *Catholic Biblical Quarterly* 26 (1964) 349–59.

Bibliography

Newsom, Carol. "Bakhtin, the Bible, and Dialogic Truth." *Journal of Religion* 76 (1996) 290–306.
North, Christopher R. *The Suffering Servant in Deutero-Isaiah: A Historical and Critical Study.* 2nd ed. London: Oxford University Press, 1963.
Nöth, Winfried. *Handbook of Semiotics.* Bloomington: Indiana University Press, 1990.
Ochs, Peter. *Peirce, Pragmatism and the Logic of Scripture.* Cambridge: Cambridge University Press, 1998.
O'Day, Gail R. "Jeremiah 9:22–23 and 1 Corinthians 1:26–31: A Study in Intertextuality." *Journal of Biblical Literature* 109 (1990) 259–67.
Orange, Donna M. *Peirce's Conception of God: A Developmental Study.* Peirce Studies 2. Lubbock, TX: Institute for Studies in Pragmaticism, 1984.
Orr, Mary. *Intertextuality: Debates and Contexts.* Cambridge, UK: Polity, 2003.
Osborne, Grant R. *The Hermeneutical Spiral: A Comprehensive Introduction to Biblical Interpretation.* 2nd ed. Downers Grove, IL: InterVarsity Academic, 2006.
Oss, D. A. "The Interpretation of the 'Stone' Passages by Peter and Paul: A Comparative Study." *Journal of the Evangelical Theological Society* 32 (1989) 181–200.
Oswalt, John N. *The Book of Isaiah: Chapters 1–39.* New International Commentary on the Old Testament. Grand Rapids: Eerdmans, 1986.
———. *The Book of Isaiah: Chapters 40–66.* New International Commentary on the Old Testament. Grand Rapids: Eerdmans, 1998.
Pearson, Sharon Clark. *The Christological and Rhetorical Properties of 1 Peter.* Studies in Bible and Early Christianity 45. Lewiston, NY: Edwin Mellen, 2001.
Perdelwitz, Richard. *Die Mysterienreligion und das Problem des I. Petrusbriefes: Ein literarischer und religionsgeschichtlicher Versuch.* Giessen: Töpelmann, 1911.
Poh, C. L. E. "The Social World of 1 Peter: Socio-Historical and Exegetical Studies." PhD diss., University of London, King's College, 1998.
Porter, Stanley E., editor. *Hearing the Old Testament in the New Testament.* Grand Rapids: Eerdmans, 2006.
Porter, Stanley E., and Jeffrey T. Reed, editors. *Discourse Analysis and the New Testament: Approaches and Results.* Journal for the Study of the New Testament Supplement Series 170. Sheffield: Sheffield Academic, 1999.
Porter, Stanley E., and Dennis L. Stamps, editors. *Rhetorical Criticism and the Bible.* Journal for the Study of the New Testament Supplement Series 195. Sheffield: Sheffield Academic, 2002.
Porter, Stanley E., and Christopher D. Stanley, editors. *As It Is Written: Studying Paul's Use of Scripture.* Atlanta: Society of Biblical Literature, 2008.
Preisker, Herbert. *Die katholischen Briefe: Erklärt von Hans Windisch.* 3rd revised ed. Tübingen: Mohr-Siebeck, 1951.
Prewitt, Terry J. *The Elusive Covenant: A Structural-Semiotic Reading of Genesis.* Bloomington: Indiana University Press, 1990.
Raees, Aisha. "Peirce's Mind." MA thesis, Southern Illinois University, 2007.
Raposa, Michael L. *Peirce's Philosophy of Religion.* Peirce Studies 5. Bloomington, IN: Indiana University Press, 1989.
Richards, E. Randolph. *Paul and First-Century Letter Writing: Secretaries, Composition and Collection.* Downers Grove, IL: InterVarsity, 2004.
Riffaterre, Michael. "Interpretation and Undecidability." *New Literary History* 12 (1981) 227–42.
———. *Semiotics of Poetry.* Bloomington: Indiana University Press, 1978.

Bibliography

———. "Syllepsis." *Critical Inquiry* 6 (1980) 625–38.
Robbins, Vernon. *Exploring the Texture of Texts: A Guide to Socio-Rhetorical Interpretation.* Harrisburg, PA: Trinity Press International, 1996.
———. *The Tapestry of Early Christian Discourse: Rhetoric, Society and Ideology.* London: Routledge, 1996.
Robin, Richard S., editor. *Annotated Catalogue of the Papers of Charles S. Peirce.* Amherst: University of Massachusetts Press, 1967.
Scheffler, Israel. *Four Pragmatists: A Critical Introduction to Peirce, James, Mead, and Dewey.* London: Routledge and Kegan Paul, 1974.
Scholes, Robert. *Semiotics and Interpretation.* New Haven: Yale University Press, 1982.
Schutter, William L. *Hermeneutic and Composition in 1 Peter.* Wissenschaftliche Untersuchungen zum Neuen Testament 30. Tübingen: Mohr Siebeck, 1989.
Selwyn, Edward Gordon. *The First Epistle of St. Peter.* London: Macmillan, 1947.
Short, T. L. *Peirce's Theory of Signs.* Cambridge: Cambridge University Press, 2007.
Snodgrass, Klyne R. "1 Peter 2:1–10: Its Formation and Literary Affinities." *New Testament Studies* 24 (1977) 97–106.
Stanley, Christopher D. *Arguing with Scripture: The Rhetoric of Quotations in the Letters of Paul.* London: T. & T. Clark, 2004.
———. "Paul and Homer: Greco-Roman Citation Practice in the First Century CE." *Novum Testamentum* 32 (1990) 48–78.
———. *Paul and the Language of Scripture: Citation Technique in the Pauline Epistles and Contemporary Literature.* Society for New Testament Studies Monograph Series 69. Cambridge: Cambridge University Press, 1992.
Stowers, Stanley K. *Letter Writing in Greco-Roman Antiquity.* Philadelphia: Westminster, 1986.
Streeter, B. H. *The Primitive Church.* London: Macmillan, 1929.
Sweeney, Marvin A. *Isaiah 1–39: With an Introduction to Prophetic Literature.* The Forms of the Old Testament Literature 16. Grand Rapids: Eerdmans, 1996.
Thiselton, Anthony C. *Hermeneutics: An Introduction.* Grand Rapids: Eerdmans, 2009.
———. *New Horizons in Hermeneutics: The Theory and Practice of Transforming Biblical Reading.* Grand Rapids: Zondervan, 1992.
———. *Thiselton on Hermeneutics: Collected Works with New Essays.* Grand Rapids: Eerdmans, 2006.
Thompson, James W. "The Rhetoric of 1 Peter." *Restoration Quarterly* 36 (1994) 237–50.
Thompson, Michael. *Clothed with Christ: The Example and Teaching of Jesus in Romans 12:1—15:13.* Journal for the Study of the New Testament Supplement Series 59. Sheffield: Sheffield Academic, 1991.
Thurén, Lauri. *Argument and Theology in 1 Peter: The Origins of Christian Paraenesis.* Journal for the Study of the New Testament Supplement Series 114. Sheffield: Sheffield Academic, 1995.
———. *The Rhetorical Strategy of 1 Peter: With Special Regard to Ambiguous Expressions.* Åbo, Finland: Åbo Academy Press, 1990.
Tobin, Yishai. *Semiotics and Linguistics.* London: Longman Group, 1990.
Torrey, C. C. *The Second Isaiah: A New Interpretation.* Edinburgh: T. & T. Clark, 1928.
Trebilco, Paul R. *Jewish Communities in Asia Minor.* Society for New Testament Studies Monograph Series 69. Cambridge: Cambridge University Press, 1991.
van Rensburg, Fika J. "The Outline of 1 Peter: A Reconsideration." *Ekklesiastikos Pharos* 74 (1992) 26–41.

Bibliography

van Rensburg, Fika J., and Steve Moyise. "Isaiah in 1 Peter 2:4–10: Applying Intertextuality to the Study of the OT in the NT." *Ekklesiastikos Pharos* 84 (2002) 12–30.

———. "Isaiah in 1 Peter 3:13–17: Applying Intertextuality to the Study of the Old Testament in the New." *Scriptura* 80 (2002) 275–86.

Watson, Duane F. *The Rhetoric of the New Testament: A Bibliographic Survey*. Tools for Biblical Study 8. Blandford Forum, UK: Deo, 2006.

———. "Rhetorical Criticism of Hebrews and the Catholic Epistles Since 1978." *Currents in Research: Biblical Studies* 5 (1997) 175–207.

Watts, John D. W. *Isaiah 1–33*. Word Biblical Commentary 24. Waco, TX: Word Books, 1985.

———. *Isaiah 34–66*. Word Biblical Commentary 25. Waco, TX: Word Books, 1987.

Watts, Rikki E. *Isaiah's New Exodus and Mark*. Wissenschaftliche Untersuchungen zum Neuen Testament 88. Tübingen: Mohr Siebeck, 1997. Reprint, *Isaiah's New Exodus in Mark*. Grand Rapids: Baker Academic, 2000.

Webb, Robert L. "The Petrine Epistles: Recent Developments and Trends." In *The Face of New Testament Studies*, edited by Scot McKnight and Grant R. Osborne, 373–90. Grand Rapids: Baker, 2004.

Webb, Robert L., and Betsy Bauman-Martin, editors. *Reading First Peter with New Eyes: Methodological Reassessments of the Letter of First Peter*. Library of New Testament Studies 364. London: T. & T. Clark, 2007.

Westermann, Claus. *Isaiah 40–66: A Commentary*. The Old Testament Library. Philadelphia: Westminster, 1969.

White, John Lee. *The Form and Function of the Body of the Greek Letter*. Society of Biblical Literature Dissertation Series 2. 2nd ed. Missoula, MT: Scholars, 1972.

———. *Light from Ancient Letters*. Philadelphia: Fortress, 1986.

———, editor. *Studies in Ancient Letter Writing*. Semeia 22. Chico, CA: Scholars, 1982.

Whitney, Gordon. "A Semiotic Approach to Old Testament Fulfillment Citations in the Fourth Gospel." Paper presented at the annual meeting of the Evangelical Theological Society, Wheaton, IL, 1988.

Williams, Jocelyn A. "A Case Study in Intertextuality: The Place of Isaiah in the 'Stone' Sayings of 1 Peter 2." *Reformed Theological Review* 66 (2007) 37–55.

Wilson, Walter T. *The Hope of Glory: Education and Exhortation in the Epistle to the Colossians*. Supplements to Novum Testamentum 88. Leiden, Brill: 1997.

Witherington, Ben, III. *Letters and Homilies for Hellenized Christians*. Vol. 2, *A Socio-Rhetorical Commentary on 1–2 Peter*. Downers Grove, IL: InterVarsity Academic, 2007.

———. *New Testament Rhetoric: An Introductory Guide to the Art of Persuasion in and of the New Testament*. Eugene, OR: Cascade, 2009.

———. *What's in the Word: Rethinking the Socio-Rhetorical Character of the New Testament*. Waco, TX: Baylor University Press, 2009.

Wittig, Susan. "A Theory of Multiple Meanings." *Semeia* 9 (1977) 75–103.

Woan, S. A. "The Use of the Old Testament in 1 Peter, with Especial Focus on the Role of Psalm 34." PhD diss., University of Exeter, 2008.

Wolf, Herbert M. *Interpreting Isaiah: The Suffering and Glory of the Messiah*. Grand Rapids: Zondervan, 1985.

Wong, Theron K. "The Use of Jesus' Sayings in 1 Peter." PhD diss., Dallas Theological Seminary, 2008.

Bibliography

Wood, Thomas R. "The Regathering of the People of God: An Investigation into the New Testament's Appropriation of the Old Testament Prophecies Concerning the Regathering of Israel." PhD diss., Trinity Evangelical Divinity School, 2006.

Wright, N. T. *The New Testament and the People of God*. Christian Origins and the Question of God 1. Minneapolis: Fortress, 1992.

Young, Robert, editor. *Untying the Text: A Post-Structuralist Reader*. Boston: Routledge & Kegan Paul, 1981.

www.ingramcontent.com/pod-product-compliance
Lightning Source LLC
Chambersburg PA
CBHW072203160426
43197CB00012B/2509